Humanitarian Intervention

Humanitarian Intervention
Moral and Philosophical Issues

Edited by Aleksandar Jokic
Introduction by Burleigh Wilkins

 broadview press

NATIONAL LIBRARY OF CANADA CATALOGUING IN PUBLICATION

Humanitarian intervention : moral and philosophical issues / edited by Aleksandar Jokic ; introduction by Burleigh Wilkins.

Includes bibliographical references.
ISBN 1-55111-489-5

1. Humanitarian intervention—Moral and ethical aspects. I. Jokić, Aleksandar

KZ6369.H84 2003   341.5'84   C2002-905698-5

Broadview Press, Ltd. is an independent, international publishing house, incorporated in 1985. Broadview believes in shared ownership, both with its employees and with the general public; since the year 2000 Broadview shares have traded publicly on the Toronto Venture Exchange under the symbol BDP.

We welcome any comments and suggestions regarding any aspect of our publications—please feel free to contact us at the addresses below, or at broadview@broadviewpress.com

North America
Post Office Box 1243,
Peterborough, Ontario,
Canada K9J 7H5
Tel: (705) 743-8990
Fax: (705) 743-8353

3576 California Road,
Orchard Park, New York
USA 14127

customerservice@broadviewpress.com
www.broadviewpress.com

United Kingdom
Thomas Lister, Ltd.
Unit 3 & 4A
Old Boundary Way,
Burscough Rd.
Ormskirk, Lancashire
L39 2YW
Tel: (01695) 575112
Fax: (01695) 570120
books@tlyster.co.uk

Australia
UNIREPS
University of
New South Wales
Sydney, NSW, 2052
Tel: + 61 2 96640999
Fax: + 61 2 96645420
info.press@unsw.edu.au

Broadview Press Ltd. gratefully acknowledges the financial support of the Government of Canada through the Book Publishing Industry Development Program for our publishing activities.

Cover design and typeset by Zack Taylor, www.zacktaylor.com.

This book is printed on acid-free paper containing 30% post-consumer fibre.

Eco-Logo Certified.
30% Post.   Printed in Canada

Contents

For Milica Djordjevic (1908-1999),
the perfect grandparent

Preface

Aleksandar Jokic

This book is one of two volumes that are the result of an ongoing project under the general name "International Law and Ethics Conference Series" (ILECS), which is concerned with exploring issues regarding the changing global order. Envisaged originally as a way of facilitating dialog between leading moral, legal, and political philosophers from the United States and Western Europe and their Eastern European counterparts, ILECS had adopted a two-part model consisting of a conference each June (since 1997) at Belgrade University and a follow-up conference in the US. Although undoubtedly operating against a background of the Anglo-American style of analytical philosophy, ILECS has sought always to reflect actively on the inter-disciplinary nature of its enterprise and to recruit experts who are not primarily philosophers.

The two volumes—one focusing on theoretical and philosophical issues, the other on the particular case of Kosovo—offer essays from 15 scholars with backgrounds in various disciplines—philosophy, international law, anthropology, political science, international studies, and Slavic studies—from different countries—United States, Yugoslavia, Germany, and Australia. The chapters are based on presentations delivered at the pair of ILECS conferences held under the title "Ethics of Humanitarian Intervention: Grounds for Internationalizing Internal Conflicts," held on June 23-25, 2000 at Belgrade University and October 13-14, 2000 at Portland State University.

The completion of the two volumes would not have been possible without financial contributions from a number of sources. The Belgrade meetings were supported by generous grants from the Open Society Foundation for Yugoslavia and Goethe Institute in Belgrade. The follow-up conference was funded by the Machette Foundation and the Conflict Resolution Graduate Program at Portland State University. The work on editing this volume was supported, in part, by the John D. and Catherine T. MacArthur Foundation.

In terms of intellectual input, it is not possible to list all those whom I wish to thank for providing valuable comments at the conferences and through other forms of communication that influenced the final shape of this volume. Special thanks are due to Dr. Robert Gould, Director of the Conflict Resolution Program at PSU, who has worked to provide a welcome venue for ILECS. Jovan Babic, my ILECS Co-Director, was involved with this project at every critical juncture. Burleigh Wilkins took on the task of writing a critical Introduction to each volume, a pleasure to read in its own right, intended to be useful to students as well as professionals by singling out a set of issues from each article for further examination. Finally, my colleagues Joseph White and Jim Chesher at the Center for Philosophical Education (CPE) at Santa Barbara City College, the official home of ILECS as the place where it originated, deserve my deep appreciation for their enduring encouragement and support.

I have certainly profited immensely from putting together this volume and engaging with its themes. I hope that it will prove to be a rich source of intellectual stimulation to advance conceptual understanding of intervention and related ideas in philosophy as well as in the other disciplines represented here.

Introduction

Burleigh Wilkins

If the "plain letter of the law" has any applicability to international law, it is this: states shall not intervene militarily or otherwise in the affairs of other states. This is stated explicitly in the Charter of the United Nations (UN). Since the UN was founded in the aftermath of World War II, the desire of member states to prevent any further interventions is understandable. An exception was provided: when a conflict within a state poses a threat to international peace, security military intervention by the UN is warranted. Indeed, the UN Charter provides for an international police force, though nothing ever came of this provision. The Charter and other UN documents also assert that human rights are to be protected, but the responsibility for the protection of human rights seems to rest on the governments of the states where the violation of these rights occurs. The prohibition of aggressive wars—i.e., wars not fought in self-defense—seems firmly established as a principle of international law, but the question of what protection if any the UN should provide to individuals when their human rights are violated by the government, or with the complicity of the government, of the country in which they live remains a contentious issue. There is the temptation to treat any human rights violations involving armed conflicts within a state as threats to international peace and security, and at times the UN Security Council has yielded to this temptation. Perhaps a more promising tact would be to regard international law as a legal system similar in many respects to municipal legal systems. Since all legal systems contain principles which under some circumstances may oppose one another, it is arguable that respect for state sovereignty and respect for human rights are two such principles. Historically the respect for state sovereignty has been allowed to trump respect for human rights, but now it has become arguable that when states fail to respect the human rights of their citizens (or others who reside within their boundaries), they may be held accountable by the UN. Intervention in a variety of forms—including, ultimately, military force—has

9

come to be regarded by some as justifiable. The question which this collection of essays addresses is this: is military humanitarian intervention justifiable and, if so, under what circumstances?

This is one of two paired volumes. The first, *Humanitarian Intervention: Moral and Philosophical Issues*, consists primarily of reflections by philosophers on the more abstract aspects of humanitarian intervention. The second, *Lessons of Kosovo: The Dangers of Humanitarian Intervention*, contains essays dealing more concretely with issues concerning the legal and moral dimensions of intervention by NATO or by the UN—all of them arguing from various points of view that the NATO intervention in Kosovo lacked clear justification, and that this raises important doubts as to the wisdom of "humanitarian" intervention in other situations.

Humanitarian Intervention as a Moral and Philosophical Issue

In "War, Revolution, and Intervention," Anthony Ellis defines humanitarian intervention broadly to include any coercive interference by a state, a group, or an individual to prevent the violation of the rights of the citizens of the state. While he justifies humanitarian intervention in the abstract, he argues that in the real world military humanitarian intervention is rarely justified. However, he also believes that wars between states are rarely justified. I have difficulty with Ellis's attempt to show that the motive behind humanitarian intervention is not important and that only the intention to perform a morally good act matters. He gives the example of someone who beats up a bully to protect an innocent person, but his motive is really to impress his girlfriend. This example has some appeal on a micro level, but what if all, or virtually all, acts of humanitarian intervention were done from selfish motives? If we were to think of humanitarian intervention as a rule-governed practice, then surely the practice would be diminished, morally speaking, if it turns out that virtually all acts of humanitarian intervention are motivated by a concern for the economic or geopolitical interests of the intervening state(s).

What is brilliant in Ellis's essay is his attempted refutation of Michael Walzer's efforts to limit the legitimacy of humanitarian intervention. While acknowledging that there is a presumption against external intervention in the domestic affairs of a state, Ellis maintains that this presumption is not strong enough to protect a state engaged in the violation of the rights of its citizens. The importance Walzer attaches to the self-determination of the state and to the autonomy of its domestic political processes is simply not warranted, according to Ellis, if that self-determination and that political process result in the violation of the rights of its citizens. The question of how a culture has come to yield certain results is less important than the question of the substantive content of these results. Ellis believes that it is far better for the individual citizens of the state to have a liberal regime thrust upon them by external intervention than for them to have an oppressive regime which is, as it were, homegrown. In the final analysis, it is the self-determination of individuals that must trump the self-determination of states. As for the idea favored by Walzer (and J.S. Mill) that a people will cherish only those freedoms which it has won for itself, this Ellis believes to be simply false.

In "Humanitarian Intervention," Burleigh Wilkins agrees with Ellis that in the real world military humanitarian intervention is rarely justified, but, unlike Ellis, Wilkins focuses on the politics of how certain states are selected as targets of humanitarian intervention. He argues that the duty of non-intervention in the affairs of a sovereign state is a *prima facie* duty, which can be overridden only when there are compelling reasons for doing so, and he believes that the questionable legality of humanitarian intervention should be resolved one way or the other by an amendment to the UN Charter. In view of the serious ideological differences which separate states, he questions the teleological model for the relations of states as destabilizing, even if the end or purpose happens to be the protection of human rights. Like Ellis, he prefers non-military forms of intervention aimed at the protection of human rights, but, apart from the mention of trade agreements, which may or may not have coercive features, he fails to elaborate on what these might be. Where the question of the autonomy of states is concerned, he can be read as occupying a position between Ellis and Jovan Babic.

In "Foreign Armed Intervention: Between Justified Aid and Illegal Violence" Jovan Babic notes an interesting difference between military intervention aimed at the protection of human rights and military intervention aimed at the defense of legal governments in need of outside help. Humanitarian intervention, understood by Babic to represent a form of military action with humanitarian justification, can only have one objective, whereas intervention in defense of a legal government allows for the defense of countries with a wide variety of values or beliefs. The examples of the latter he offers are South Vietnam, and Afghanistan in the 1980s, indicating the uncertain value of interventions justified by the government-defense criterion. In an essay written with real moral eloquence Babic depicts humanitarian intervention as a kind of fanaticism aimed at imposing a particular "value matrix" not only on a given state but eventually on the entire world. This is entirely at odds with the presumed values of tolerance invested in existing concepts of sovereignty of national states and in the regulative idea of principled equality of all states.

Humanitarian intervention, thus, is aimed not at the protection of any established rights but at a creation of a new world order in which the rights of sovereign states will be sacrificed on the altar of what happened to be an American conception of what is for the common good. The outcome, easily imagined, is a militarization of the world, and a decline of the civil character of authority governments normally enjoy. This whole scheme can bring about justified fear from becoming labeled as "showing insufficient allegiance to human rights." For, it can lead to isolation, rogue state status, or even being selected as target for military action. The normative idea of an "international community" becomes an idea of a club, membership in which is desired just because it can protect one from such a threat. Instead of being only a justified exception, based on strong reasons to abandon ex quo *ante* prohibition against intervening—and thus becoming a form of duty—resort to intervention would increasingly become the favored means for realizing a unified world defined in terms of the ideals of human rights and democracy. For Babic this would be a strange outcome as it would impose as a law something that could no longer be conceived as "our law" in any meaningful way. The latter, however, is a necessary condition without which no law can have any validity, according to Babic.

The picture is further complicated when Babic makes the claim that a state unwilling, incapable or incompetent in administering its own laws cannot be tolerated. This corroborates his thesis that the plausible justification for an act of intervention must come from outside the scope of the narrowly construed humanitarian considerations. But who is in a better position to intervene, a neighbor familiar with the history and culture in the target state or a distant and presumably less knowledgeable superpower? What is characteristic of a superpower, according to Babic, is a pursuit of some larger scale ideal that always makes it easy for many relevant items pertaining to local history and culture to become of no significance. For this reason Babic gives preference to neighboring states as intervening parties. However, this raises several questions. Are governments legitimate if they "fit" the history and culture of a people even if this history reflects systematic rights violations? Is there a presumption that the rights of sovereign states trump the rights of their citizens, a presumption which can be overridden only in extreme cases, e.g., Uganda and East Pakistan? Why are neighboring states so epistemically privileged that only they, and not some distant superpower, can determine that human rights violations by a sovereign state are sufficient to warrant a humanitarian intervention?

One interesting point Babic makes is that the *prima facie right* of intervention grows out of an exception to the principled prohibition of intervention. Having a right of intervention implies a very strong justification, which according to Babic means that where there is an actual *right* of intervention there is also a *duty* of intervention. I don't think this is true, but it highlights the problem of determining the purpose of asserting that there is a right of intervention. If the grounds for intervention are so strong as to override the duty of non-intervention, is it still morally permissible for the would-be intervener(s) to choose not to intervene? Can the costs of intervention justify the choice not to intervene in cases of horrendous rights violations?

"Humanitarian Intervention and Moral Theory" by Michael Philips is in many ways the most difficult paper in this collection, but it merits very close attention. Relying on his book *Between Universalism and Skepticism* (Oxford, 1994), Philips raises questions about the nature of morality itself and applies the results to humanitarian intervention. He distinguishes between a "metaphysical conception" of morality and an "instrumental conception." He maintains that this distinction cannot be mapped onto the familiar distinction between deontological and consequential theories of morality, and he maintains that there can be deontological and consequentialist versions of the metaphysical conception of morality as well as of the instrumental conception. What is important for us here is his claim that the two different conceptions yield quite different approaches to the problem of humanitarian intervention. The metaphysical conception will focus on philosophical questions such as the moral worth of individuals, and the instrumental conception will focus upon empirical questions such as the effects of humanitarian intervention upon the relations of states. Since the two different conceptions are not in themselves theories, nothing "follows" from them in the way in which principles of action may be said to follow from philosophical theories. Philips acknowledges his preference for the instrumental conception of morality, but he is willing to grant that there can be instrumental reasons for and against humanitarian intervention.

In "Preempting Humanitarian Intervention," Thomas Pogge suggests an approach that would reduce or eliminate situations that give rise to demands for humanitarian intervention. He proposes that we focus upon the framework of international laws, treaties, and conventions within which governments and other powerful agents interact. According to Pogge, we need an institutional understanding of a human right to X as "the demand that every society ... ought to be so organized that all of its participants enjoy secure access to X." He seeks to diffuse the charge that this is parochial and Western by saying that not every human right needs to be legally guaranteed. He believes that even those who are hostile to "a legal rights culture" could share in the goal of establishing for all humans a secure access to certain vital goods. He thinks that the institutional understanding of human rights would single out the truly essential elements of "human flourishing" and avoid "any conceptual connection with legal rights." I have some doubts about this. First, what is truly essential to human flourishing may be just what is at issue between Western and communitarian or Asian conceptions of human rights. Second, while we can grant Pogge his conceptual point that not every human right must be linked to some constitutional or legal right, there is strong empirical reason to link the efficacy of human rights proclamations to effective legal protections. On the level of practical reform Pogge is, I think, more persuasive: let there be constitutional provisions that future governments not be obligated to repay loans incurred by undemocratic or unconstitutional predecessor regimes. Such a provision would make it less attractive for would-be putschists to attempt to overthrow a democratic regime. Even here, however, I have some doubts. The longer a regime established by putschists lasts and the more stable it becomes, the greater may be the inclination of international bankers to lend it money; even in the case of shaky regimes, banks may make loans, although at extremely high interest rates. The governments of other countries may be committed to not pressuring a newly restored democratic regime to pay off loans undertaken by a previous undemocratic regime, but international bankers may still insist on repayment before making any new loans. Finally, there is the question of why non-democratic forces might seek to overthrow a democratic regime in the first place. In some instances economic motives may be dominant, but in other cases there may be a genuine difference over what counts as essential to human flourishing. An undemocratic regime—and here Afghanistan under the rule of the Taliban comes to mind—may be willing to sacrifice considerable economic well-being for what it perceives as the spiritual or moral well-being of its people, and such a regime may be relatively indifferent to the kinds of pressure Pogge has in mind. Still Pogge's proposal may have merit in a significant number of cases, and it should be read as part of a story which is still unfolding, a story of how a complex and subtle tweaking of municipal and international law can help prevent the tragic circumstances that give rise to calls for humanitarian intervention.

Alfred Rubin in "Humanitarian Intervention" denies that there is such an entity as "the international community" and argues that in most circumstances the UN lacks the legal authority to intervene militarily to prevent human rights abuses. His two points are intertwined. Community presupposes agreement, and Rubin maintains that such agreement does not exist. He reminds us that the majority of states are not liberal democracies and that there simply is no universal consensus on a host of basic issues including, for example, what is to count as murder. Rubin considers himself to be a "fallibilist," and as such he raises the question of who among us is qualified to determine the content of natural law morality and its applicability to international law.

Rubin astutely points out that some of the most cherished human rights documents are not legally binding at all and that enforcement is left up to the signatory states. For example, the Genocide Convention leaves intervention up to "a competent tribunal of the state in the territory in which the act was committed" or else to "a competent international tribunal" whose jurisdiction has been accepted by the contracting parties. Rubin also argues that in some of its interventions the Security Council has wrongly claimed that it is acting on the authority of Chapter VII of the UN Charter, which is concerned with what action should be taken with respect to threats to peace, breaches of peace, and acts of aggression; in any event he is troubled by the role that political considerations play in Security Council decisions concerning intervention.

Unlike most contributors to this volume, Rubin spells out several alternatives to military intervention. His principal strategy is what he calls "exposure and embarrassment." For example, the Helsinki Accords, although not even a treaty, helped end some human rights abuses in Eastern Europe. Sometimes municipal law can be effective, as in the Sullivan Rules which the US imposed on American firms seeking to do business with apartheid South Africa. And, although he does not mention this in the present essay, he has elsewhere praised the European Court of Human Rights as an effective tool for protecting the rights of individuals. I greatly admire Rubin's hard-nosed approach to international law, but I am troubled by the following considerations. If there is, as Rubin believes, no international community and no consensus on what is to count as a human right, under what circumstances would his strategy of "exposure and embarrassment" be applicable? Why would a state be embarrassed if it were exposed for a violation of an alleged human right if that state did not believe in human rights or at least not in the human right in question? Might not any embarrassment be purely political and not moral? And for that matter might not the decision as to what abuses should be exposed become politicized, much as Rubin has complained that Security Council decisions about intervention are politicized?

If, as the majority of the contributors to the second volume to arise out of these conferences believe, NATO intervention in Kosovo was illegal, what is the moral significance of this? In "From Nuremberg to Kosovo: The Morality of Illegal International Legal Reform," Allen Buchanan considers the possibility that an illegal act done for the purpose of creating a new norm of international law may be morally defensible. Certainly it has been efficacious in the past: consider, for example, Britain's illegal search and seizure of ships flying the flags of other states as a means to ending the transatlantic slave trade. Even if NATO's attack on Serbia were illegal, might it not have served a similarly laudable purpose if it contributed to the creation of new norms of international law which would justify humanitarian intervention to protect human rights?

In the most original and exciting part of his paper, Buchanan provides eight "guidelines" for assessments of illegal acts aimed at the moral improvement of a system such as the UN. Here I will give just two examples of these guidelines (which are not to be confused with a set of necessary conditions): "Other things being equal, the less seriously defective the system is from the standpoint of substantive justice, the greater the burden of justification for illegal acts," and "Other things being equal, the more likely it is that the illegal act will actually contribute to a significant moral improvement in the system the stronger the case for committing it."

How does NATO intervention in Kosovo fare under the guidelines proposed by Buchanan? In some respects Buchanan believes it fares well, especially since the protection of human rights can be seen as a core value internal to the UN. But NATO intervention can be read in one of two ways: either as a morally justifiable departure from the rule that Security Council authorization is required for intervention, a rule which despite its defects is desirable, or as an illegal act aimed at replacing Security Council authorization with a new rule empowering regional defense alliances to engage in intervention at their discretion. Read in the second way, NATO intervention is an implausible candidate for being an illegal act aimed at the reform of the UN. Would we, Buchanan asks, be willing to allow a military alliance of China and Pakistan to intervene in Kashmir to protect the rights of Muslims?

In the spirit of Buchanan's proposed guidelines, I believe, however, that there is a third possible reading of the NATO intervention which would allow regional military alliances to engage in intervention *not* "at their discretion" but if and only if their intervention satisfies certain criteria. Such criteria might include the following: peaceful diplomatic resolutions of the problem in question have failed; the intervention will respect the principle of proportionality; and the intervention can reasonably be expected to succeed in a fairly short period of time. A regional military alliance which acted in violation of these criteria could be condemned by the UN, and (since we are talking about a reformed UN) a continued violation or a pattern of violations could lead to the outlawing of such an organization. Some interventions, like some wars, could be branded as "acts of aggression."

I

War, Revolution, and Humanitarian Intervention

Anthony Ellis

Introduction

There are two separate, but connected, sets of questions that we must address. One is about what the *legal* status should be of war, revolution, and humanitarian intervention. The other is concerned with the *moral* status of these actions.

Armed revolution is not illegal in international law.[1] War is, of course, illegal, except in self-defense, but the right of self-defense is typically interpreted very broadly. By contrast, international law, and most theorists, have taken a very restrictive view of humanitarian intervention, armed intervention in particular.[2]

As for morality, I shall not guess at what the prevalent views may be. But many people think that there is a strong moral presumption against humanitarian intervention of a quite different sort from the moral presumption against war and revolution.

My aim in this paper is to suggest that we, and international law in particular, should think more similarly about war, revolution, and intervention. The result, I suggest, would be that, although most forms of intervention would be easier to justify, armed intervention would be very much harder to justify because the use of armed force in international relations generally is much harder to justify than is typically thought.

Definition

I shall define humanitarian intervention in the following way. A humanitarian intervention occurs when a state, or a group, or an individual, interferes coercively in the affairs of a foreign state in order to prevent the violation of the rights of the citizens of that state. This is inevitably a little vague; let me clarify one or two points.

An intervention is *coercive* in that it is intended to change things against the will of the governing body. Thus, it includes many things other than the use of military force, such as sanctions, covert operations, and the funding of opposition groups. But it does not include attempts to change the government's mind by rational argument.[3]

The *target* of intervention does not have to be the government of the state in question; it may be aimed at groups that the government should, but cannot, control.

Equally, my definition allows that agents other than states may intervene. It makes a legal difference whether an agent that interferes in the affairs of a foreign state is itself a state, or a body like Amnesty International, or an individual. There may be good reason for such intervention in law, but morally, in my view, it is all the same.

It is important to note that in order for an intervention to be *humanitarian*, it need not have humanitarian *motives*. Writers seem generally to have thought that it must.[4] However, this is an important mistake.[5] When we judge an *action* as opposed to an *agent*, the *intention* is important but the *motive* is usually irrelevant.[6] If I intervene when I see a bully hurting a small child, this action is right, and an action to be encouraged, even if my only motive is the desire to impress my girlfriend. Similarly, if a nation intervenes when a state oppresses some of its citizens, it may be motivated by, say, revenge, or self-interest, but so long as it acts with the intention to stop the oppression (and, of course, no other wrong intention) then this does not alter the justifiability of the act, though of course it will affect our estimate of the moral quality of the nation. It would be absurd to suggest that the brutal Vietnamese regime which ousted Pol Pot was acting out of humanitarian motives; still, it acted rightly in ousting Pol Pot. Tanzania, too, had self-interested motives when it invaded Uganda (though there is little doubt that President Nyerere was also motivated by a humanitarian concern); if so, this might reflect on the moral quality of Tanzania, but not on the moral correctness of its action.

This is important, because there is little hope that in the foreseeable future states will intervene wholly or even primarily out of humanitarian motives. Our central concern should be with judging the actions of states, deciding which actions are to be allowed and which to be prohibited, as opposed to judging the moral quality of states.

The Falkland Islands

According to the doctrine that we inherited from the nineteenth century, states had in international law more or less unfettered right to go to war;[7] by contrast, they had virtually no right to intervene in the domestic affairs of other states, however gruesome those affairs might be. All that has changed, of course,[8] but we are left with a residue. In international law, and international theorizing generally, it is thought much harder to justify an intervention than a self-defensive war or a revolution. Legally, a country may go to war to defend itself against some relatively trivial aggression—stolen, but worthless, land, for instance. It may go to war to help another nation defend itself against such aggression. But it may not intervene to protect a population suffering equivalent oppression by its own government.

Let us take an example. In 1982, the United Kingdom went to war to repel an Argentinean invasion of the Falkland Islands. Given that Argentina had no legitimate claim to the Falklands—I shall assume this for the sake of the argument[9]—this was an act of self-defense within international law.[10] And it was fairly generally approved of; it was supported by the European nations and by the US, though the Organization of American States (OAS) supported Argentina.

What moral justification was there for this action, in which almost 1,000 people lost their lives?

The UK had no significant strategic or resource interests in the Islands, so there were only two possible moral justifications for the action.[11] One was that the people who lived on the Islands overwhelmingly wanted to be ruled by the UK rather than Argentina. Now, I think it important to say that whether one is ruled by one state rather than another comparable one (Eire rather than the United Kingdom, say) is not, in itself, a question over which it is legitimate to spill blood. Of course, other things may be involved. In the present case, the Argentine government had been for some time a particularly brutal one, and there seemed little reason to expect better of General Galtieri, so the states were not comparable, and this may have been sufficient to make the difference. In any case, let us assume for now that this would have been an adequate justification.

The UK put forward a second justification: it claimed that the Falklands were its territory. What force does this have? In international law, a country may certainly go to war to protect its territory against aggression. But, as far as morality is concerned, the issue is not so clear. In a war, people generally lose their lives, and the mere protection of a piece of land will not, in and of itself, justify that. The land may have important strategic significance or vital resources, and then the issue may be different, but that was not so in the case of the Falklands; therefore, this was not an adequate moral justification. However, a country's defense of its own land can also be brought under the rubric of upholding international law, or upholding a general norm against aggression. If the UK's claim to the Falklands was reasonably clear, then this might be a second and, in my view, very strong justification.

Imagine that history had gone differently. Imagine that in 1774, when Britain left West Falkland, she had ceded the territory to Spain and that when Argentina became independent, the Falklands had become Argentinean territory and had been ruled effectively by Argentina. Let us also imagine that the British settlers on the Falklands remained as a distinct, but reasonably satisfied, minority community until, let us say, the 1960s when, for whatever reason, they became an oppressed minority, subject to just the sort of civil rights abuses to which the citizens of Argentina were subject under General Galtieri in 1982. Eventually, let us imagine, the UK government, at the request of the local Falklands administration, invades the Falklands and declares that it will administer the territory until there is solid assurance that the inhabitants will be properly treated. Or imagine that the Islanders' response to the oppression was a wish to secede to the UK, and the UK invaded the islands and took them over.

Given the scale of the oppression that we are imagining, an invasion in either of these cases would certainly have been in violation of international law and would have been almost universally condemned in the international community.[12] My question is how we can justify what actually happened and yet condemn these imaginary actions. What is the relevant difference that justifies this difference of response? My answer is that there is none and that we cannot justify the actual war but condemn the fictitious intervention.

Of course, the actual action could, as I have said, be justified as upholding international law, and the imaginary invasion could not, at present, be justified in this way; this would generally be a relevant and important consideration. However, that would not be an answer to our present question, since, of course, precisely what we need to know is whether international law should indeed prohibit the one action but allow the other.

How, then, can it be held that the actual action was morally justifiable, and the law that legitimated it justifiable, but the imaginary action not? What is so special about intervention?

The Arguments

There are consequentialist and non-consequentialist answers to our question. The former claim that interventions always, or generally, lead to bad consequences, or—differently—that a permissive rule governing interventions would itself do so; presumably, wars and revolutions are thought to be different. By contrast, non-consequentialist replies argue that interventions are unjustified for reasons having nothing to do with their consequences. I shall start with the latter first.

What, then, is special about interventions?

NON-CONSEQUENTIALIST ARGUMENTS

Obviously, in one sense what is special about interventions is their violation of national sovereignty. But the right of non-intervention is nine-tenths of national sovereignty.[13] So, if the right of non-intervention is questioned, it will hardly help to answer that question by appealing to the right of sovereignty. What has to be argued is that the package that we call "national sovereignty" should include the right to non-intervention, understood in the restrictive way that is now current.

The argument that is most often given for this proposition is a consequentialist one based upon the alleged success of the Westphalian system in keeping international order. I shall return to this claim in passing, but for the moment it is non-consequentialist arguments with which we are concerned.

It would surely be impossible to mount a plausible non-consequentialist argument for an *absolute* prohibition on interventions, for it may seem that there must be *some* limits on how a government may treat its own people before it is legitimate for outsiders to intervene — that seems to be simply an extension of the principle that individuals have a legitimate interest in (some of) the affairs of others. We are not required to stand idly by while our neighbor murders his family, nor even while he buys the gun to do it, nor even while he sinks into the pathology that leads him to do it. Within certain limits, morality requires us, and certainly permits us, to intervene. So, too, does self-interest: a neighbor with the potential to murder his family is not a safe neighbor. It could, of course, be held that one's legitimate interest in the affairs of others stops at national boundaries, but, so far as I know, no-one takes this utterly implausible view. Obviously, the complications involved in a state intervening in the affairs of another state are greater than those involved in intervening in the affairs of one's neighbor, but that does not alter the principle at stake.

However, it may be possible to mount a non-consequentialist argument for a strict, though not absolute prohibition. That is the position of Michael Walzer.

Walzer is not an absolutist about the right of a state to treat its citizens as it sees fit (in his latest contribution, he seems to suggest that it at least must not be "murderous").[14] According to Walzer, intervention may be permissible, but only if:

1. a state has more than one community, or is an empire and one community within it is fighting for independence; or

2. the intervention is a counter-intervention in civil war; or

3. the government of the state being intervened in is involved in massacre, enslavement, or mass expulsion of its population.[15]

Here is his argument in six stages.

1. Walzer's argument depends upon distinguishing what he calls internal legitimacy from external legitimacy. A state is *internally* legitimate if there is a "union" or "fit" between the government and the people.[16] That is to say, the government "represents the political life of its people,"[17] the "people is governed in accordance with its own traditions,"[18] the type of government comes to the people "as it were, naturally, reflecting a widely shared world view or way of life."[19]

External legitimacy, by contrast, is the *presumption* of internal legitimacy, a presumption that must stand so long as it is not "radically apparent" that the government does not represent the political life of the people (as where the government practices mass enslavement or mass murder, for instance).

2. If a government has no internal legitimacy, if it does not fit its people, they have a right to rebel. But:

3. If a people have a right to rebel, then they also have a right not to rebel, "because they ... judge rebellion to be imprudent or uncertain of success or because they ... still believe the government to be tolerable, or they are accustomed to it, or they are personally loyal to its leaders."[20]

4. If a people choose not to rebel, and we then intervene, we have usurped their rights.

5. If, on the other hand, they choose to rebel, foreigners have no need, and therefore, again, no right, to intervene.[21]

6. If a government simply lacks internal legitimacy, then intervention will be unjustified. All that could justify an intervention is external illegitimacy, a state in which it is manifest that the government does not represent the political life of the people.

I believe that all six of these propositions are mistaken.

1. First, the account of internal legitimacy is unacceptable: a government may oppress its people and still represent "the political life of the people," for the oppression of minorities—or majorities, for that matter—may have been an accepted part of the history of a nation (as with Untouchability in pre-independence India, for instance). In such circumstances there may be pragmatic

reasons to regard the government as the "legitimate" government in international law—to accept it into the UN, for instance—but its oppressive nature may be sufficient to prevent us from regarding it as legitimate in any other way.

2. "If a government does not fit its people, they have a right to rebel." That will depend upon the "political life" of the people that the government fails to represent. A people with a history of oppression of minorities does not, for instance, have a right to rebel against a government that seeks to end that repression merely because the government no longer "fits" the people.

3. "If a people have a right to rebel, then they also have a right not to rebel."

An oppressed people may indeed sometimes have a right not to rebel, but that does not follow simply from their having a right to do so, any more than it follows from the fact that I have a right to support my family that I also have a right not to support them. In certain circumstances, there may be a duty to rebel.

Nor, I should think it obvious, does their having a right not to rebel follow from their being "accustomed" to the government and "personally loyal to its leaders."

4. "If a people have a right not to rebel, and choose not to do so, and we then intervene, we have usurped their rights."

This depends upon what sort of right they have.

Imagine a family in which one family member constantly abuses another, a young child; the only effective solution would be to report the abusive member to the law, but the other family members resist this because, as is often the case, in an ambivalent way they feel a "personal loyalty" to the abusive member. Some might hold that in this morally conflicted situation, though they will have a duty to work within the family to mitigate the abuse, they have a right not to report it. But, if so, the right here is, I believe, merely a Hohfeldian "privilege,"[22] and it does not follow from their having such a right that others may not intervene. To have such a right is merely not to have a duty to report the abuse; this does not imply that others also have a duty not to report it.

The same point emerges in a different scenario. When a government oppresses a minority, the majority may have a right not to resist this because the cost to them would be too great. But the right here is, again, merely a Hohfeldian "privilege," and, again, it does not follow from their having such a right that others may not intervene, even if the intervention would impose the same cost on the majority as rebellion would have imposed. Individuals may have, though some would deny this, a right to protect their own welfare at some cost to others, but others are not always required to respect that right.[23]

5. "If a people choose to rebel, foreigners have no need, and therefore no right, to intervene."

The claim that a people has no need of assistance if it does choose to rebel is surely false; there is no guarantee that a popular uprising will be successful in a reasonable time and at reasonable cost.

6. "The right to intervene depends not upon whether a state has internal legitimacy, but upon its external legitimacy, that is, the presumption of internal legitimacy. And that presumption will stand so long as a state does not engage in massacre, enslavement, or mass expulsion."

If the previous five propositions are mistaken, then so is the sixth.

In any case, it is surely curious. After all, why should there be any such *presumption* at all, let alone such a strong one? Walzer himself remarks that "countries with tyrannical governments make up the greater part of international society."[24] Why assume anything in advance of the evidence, let alone in the face of it?

Walzer suggests that we do not know enough about foreign nations to know in general whether their governments "fit" them.[25] But this seems bewilderingly pessimistic. It is not just egregious regimes such as those of Idi Amin or Pol Pot whose lack of "fit" is apparent. On the contrary. One did not need to know much about the true state of affairs in order to know, for instance, that the Soviet regime in Poland when Walzer wrote his article did not properly represent the Polish people.

Walzer also says that it is a "morally necessary" presumption. Perhaps the thought is that the presumption is morally necessary because it is "simply the respect that foreigners owe to a historic community and to its internal life."[26] But any reasonable pluralism should accept that some cultures are worthy of respect and others are not, and that in general we can judge which are which.

Perhaps the thought is different. Perhaps "morally necessary" means "necessary if we are to have any morally acceptable dealings with other states." Here is an analogy: one might perhaps say that it is morally necessary to presume, until there is contrary evidence, that other people are trustworthy if we are to have morally acceptable relations with them. This may be true, but the analogy with states is weak. Personal relations largely require the absence of rationalistic calculations in one's day-to-day dealings with others. But inter-state relations are not personal relations. Rationalistic calculation is their proper mode.

Here is another way of thinking of the matter, but one on which it hardly seems appropriate to talk of a *moral* necessity, and which, in reality, generates only a consequentialist argument. We want other states, or most of them anyway, to be members of the international community, independently of what their internal policies are like; that is not possible so long as each state holds open the possibility of interfering in the internal affairs of other states, because it is not in the interest of states, weaker ones in particular, to enter into a community in which that is the general presumption.

However, we must be careful about speaking of what is in a *state's* interests, for this could mean different things. We may think of the state as the union of people and government, but we may also think of it differently, as when, for instance, we speak of the state oppressing its people. Now, an arrangement that is in the interest of the state in the second sense may not be in the interest of the state in the first sense, and the question we should be concerned with is what is in the interest of the state in the first sense. In this sense it is not so clear that a less restrictive rule on intervention would not be in the interest of (most) states, for a less restrictive rule would, in principle, offer citizens some degree of protection against their own governments—a not inconsiderable matter in many parts of the world. Would it not, however, put them at risk of aggressive states acting under cover of humanitarian intervention? This seems unlikely. First, in general, aggressive states do not need such a cover. Second, it depends upon what the rule would be. No-one suggests that there should be a blanket permission for intervention whenever a state disapproves of the internal affairs of another state. There may be stringent requirements short of what are presently accepted.

Of course, it may be that most states would not in fact join an international organization in which states were given a less restrictive right of intervention. That may well be true. The question at issue at present, however, is whether they have a good reason for that stance. I think that they do not. (How to convince them of this is another question on which I have nothing much to say.)

Underlying Walzer's argument is the great weight he places on "the political process" which itself, he says, constitutes self-determination, holding that it "also has value" along with the end-state to which it leads.[27]

This is, of course, analogous to a familiar type of reason when we are discussing interventions into the life of an individual. At its center is the idea that it is not only the way one's life is that matters, but also the way in which one arrived at that life, and it is a strong argument against the more simplistic type of utilitarianism. It has less force, though still some,[28] against more sophisticated versions, which allow that weight can be given not only to end-states but also to the processes that lead to them. However, its application to the political arena is problematic. Talk of self-determination in the individual case is relatively straightforward: an individual determines his own life, and we attach value to that. In the political arena, however, self-determination is something different: when a *community* "determines its own life," some *individuals* do indeed determine their own lives, but they also determine the lives of others, and that is not something that has value. It may be far better for a country to have a liberal regime thrust upon it—if it is possible, which is perhaps rarely so[29]—rather than to arrive at an oppressive regime by its own means. That will depend on how oppressive it is, and what the costs of thrusting a liberal regime on it may be.

Walzer writes, revealingly, that people "have a right to a state in which their rights are violated."[30] That will be so when this has been arrived at by what he calls "domestic politics" engaging in processes which honestly express the local culture. However, I think that the claim, when not interpreted in a way which deprives it of actual application, is a false and dangerous one. We may agree that *individuals* have a right to be oppressed if they wish (voluntarily to sell themselves into slavery, for instance). And if Walzer's claim were merely that, if a people *unanimously* desired to have an oppressive state then they have a right to it, we need not cavil. But that cannot be what he means. Oppressive states never have the support of all who are subject to them—even if we think that they have the support of those whom they oppress. Apart from any other consideration, such states include children, who are not able to decide whom to support and do not even know that they are being oppressed; such states make institutional arrangements that future generations will inherit whether they wish to or not. So we must be speaking of a people's right to a state that violates the rights even of those citizens who do not support it. Now, no group of people can have that right. In my view, the moral rights of groups are wholly reducible to the rights of their individual members; that is the only way in which groups can have moral rights.[31] If that is correct, then we should say that no individual has a right to a state in which people are oppressed, for no-one has a right that others be oppressed, except in special, irrelevant circumstances. If, on the other hand, it is not correct, and a people can indeed possess a right—as a people—we should still get the same result; a group certainly does not have a right to a state in which some of its members are oppressed (except, again, in special and irrelevant circumstances) because no group has a right to oppress any of its members. No-one has a right to oppress anyone, and the most exalted view of the ontological status of groups should not deny that.

If there is some reason why other states should not coercively intervene in the affairs of an oppressive state, then I think that they must be reasons having to do with the likely consequences of such interventions, not with the intrinsic value of a state's self-determination.

CONSEQUENTIALIST ARGUMENTS

The UN General Assembly Resolution 2131 (XX); § 5 says:

> Every state has an inalienable right to choose its political, economic, social and cultural systems, without interference in any form by another state. [This was subsequently incorporated into GAOR 2625 on Friendly Relations; see Resolution 36/103 for a detailed list of prohibited activities.]

Despite the absolute nature of this prohibition, it is in fact backed by consequentialist reasoning:

> The strict observance of these obligations is an essential condition to ensure that nations live together in peace with one another, since the practice of any form of intervention not only violates the spirit and letter of the United Nations but also leads to the creation of situations which threaten international peace and security. (§ 4)

Consequentialist reasoning can, of course, generate absolute prohibitions, but only in rather special circumstances, as when, for instance, the act of foreclosing options itself has greater utility than would allowing oneself to calculate the consequences of each option. There seems little reason to think that this is the case with interventions in the international arena. Almost everybody thinks that the interventions in Cambodia, Uganda, and the Central African Republic, for instance, achieved considerable utility. It is consistent to hold that strict observance of a rule prohibiting them would have yielded yet greater utility, but some reason would need to be given for this claim. One possible reason might be that an absolute prohibition would deter states from aggression, since they would no longer be able to justify their actions by claiming that they were justifiable humanitarian interventions allowed by international law. This is far-fetched. States bent on aggression pay little heed to the niceties of international law; when they do so, they in any case usually justify themselves by claiming that they are acting in self-defense—a relatively easy claim to make given the current nature of international law. In this respect, at least, there seems little reason to differentiate between military interventions and other sorts of war.

A credible rule of law, then, will recognize *some* circumstances in which it is legitimate to intervene. The only question is what they are.

In fact, of course, most people do not hold an absolutist position. They hold that humanitarian interventions can be justified, but only in the most exigent circumstances (where there is the likelihood of mass murder or mass enslavement, for instance). They hold this because they think that, with interventions—as opposed to self-defensive wars, presumably—there is too little likelihood of success at an acceptable cost. What is the argument for this?

It might be said that, in the world as we know it, this is inevitable—it is simply in the nature of interventions. Interventions, after all, are never clean and easy. For one thing, there is likely to be significant loss of life, for the nation that is being intervened in will probably offer forceful resistance. For another, the course of the action will be largely unpredictable. We cannot know, for instance, the possibility of counter-intervention, perhaps leading to wider warfare. And there is also the danger of "mission creep," a fear which gripped American foreign policy after Vietnam, gained renewed energy after Somalia, and which required the events of September 11, 2001 to overcome it. And then it is, of course, often difficult for a state to extract itself from a nation into which it has intervened. So, interventions should be avoided in all but the most demanding cases.

But these considerations apply to all warfare and are not usually taken to generate an almost complete prohibition on it. Let us remember that almost 1000 people lost their lives in the Falklands conflict. The conflict did not lead to wider warfare, but that may be because the UK won a resounding victory much more quickly than had been widely expected. It is hard to know what would have happened if the conflict had gone on for a significantly longer period. Chile and Argentina were already in dispute about territory, for instance, which was undoubtedly why Chile gave some support to the UK. And that is not a point about the particular conflict, but about armed force generally in international affairs. When Britain declared war on Germany in 1939, it was not envisaged that this would eventually involve the Soviet Union, Japan, and the US, or that 50 million people would lose their lives and countless millions would be displaced, or that a divided Germany would become the potential battleground for a massive conflict between the USSR and NATO. And, of course, a nation can certainly have difficulty in exiting—with decency—from an intervention, but that can happen in warfare too.

A second argument appeals to the actual history of interventions, which has been, it may be alleged, spectacularly bad. Here, certain disastrous examples immediately spring to mind—for instance, Vietnam and Somalia.[32]

We need to be careful here about what we count as success and failure. The civil order that followed Tanzania's relatively straightforward invasion of Uganda was fairly awful,[33] but it was surely better than what had obtained under the monstrous lunatic Idi Amin which it displaced. Nor did the French coup in the Central African Republic in 1979 usher in an era of peace and security, but what followed was surely better than what had preceded it and certainly worth the cost (the incompetent and brutal Jean-Bedel Bokassa was deposed by the French in a bloodless coup). And we might say the same about Vietnam's intervention into Cambodia under the Khmer Rouge.

In any case, the history of war and revolution has not been good either. And here again we should remind ourselves to think about what we count as a success in an armed conflict. Since 1945 there have been around 200 serious armed conflicts in the world. I should guess that virtually none of them has achieved any good for either side substantially greater than could have been achieved by other means. Take, for instance, the present war in Sri Lanka. It is hard to see what justifies the position of either side. The Tamils no longer have any very strong reason for having an independent state—and certainly not one good enough to justify the more than 63,000 deaths that the war has caused—nor do the Sinhalese have any very strong reason for denying them one. Even in those cases in which it is generally considered to have been justifiable to have gone to war, as in World War II and the Gulf War, things are not straightforward; in both cases, though particularly in the case of World War II, the harm involved was huge, and there is serious question as to whether roughly equal benefits might not eventually have been achieved by other means. Of course, World War II was a success for the Allies in the sense that the Nazi regime was beaten. However, if the measure of success is taken to be something wider—say, the securing of a stable, peaceful, and prosperous Europe at reasonable cost—then things look different. To repeat, 50 million people lost their lives in the course of that war, countless millions were injured and countless millions displaced. It is, of course, impossible to know what the course of history would have been if Poland, Britain, and France had not resisted Hitler by military means, but it is hard to believe that, if the actual outcome had been known in advance, some other alternative would not have been chosen.

This is not to say, of course, that nations should simply acquiesce in aggression, for there are other possible responses than military force. Some of these will include violence and loss of life, but that is a different thing from war. Nor is it to say that nations should never go to war. Aggression should be resisted not only in self-defense, but also to uphold international law. In either case, benefits and costs must be kept in reasonable balance, and I suggest that this has rarely been the case in wars during this century. They have been kept in balance in the classic cases of intervention at least as well as in the ordinary wars.

Here is a third argument: it may be said that intervening in the affairs of another state, even with a strong justification, will tend to lead other nations to intervene in the domestic affairs of other nations, perhaps without such a good cause and that this effect will outweigh any good one may do.

However, one should not appeal to precedent effects without carefully weighing both sides of the balance. On the one side we have a somewhat speculative and remote effect: because a nation has intervened in the affairs of another state, in rather special circumstances, other nations will generally be more inclined to intervene in the affairs of other states and may do so when there is insufficient justification. On the other side of the balance, however, we may have the immediate threat of serious harm to actual people. In such circumstances, one cannot simply assume that the former will outweigh the latter, nor even that it will do so in all but the most serious cases.

In any case the argument is double-edged. *Not* intervening may have a precedent effect too, encouraging nations to think that they can oppress their own citizens with impunity. There is no *a priori* reason why one of these effects should be thought to outweigh the other. Again, it will require a careful weighing of the circumstances in each particular case. Here, it may be worth remarking that the most urgent thing to provide a deterrence against is not intervention in the affairs of other nations, for which there are many disincentives already, nor genocide, which is happily rare, but the violations of human rights which are more or less routine over large parts of Asia and Africa.

The foregoing argument focused on the alleged consequences of actual interventions. A different argument focuses not on the results of particular interventions—on that the argument may be neutral—but on the alleged consequences of adopting a less restrictive rule on intervention in international law; the result, it is said, would be that states would use the excuse of humanitarian intervention in order to aggress against other states and that this would outweigh any good that the less restrictive rule might lead to.

It is no doubt true that states would justify acts of aggression in this way. Indeed, they already do so. But we could mount exactly the same argument against allowing states the right to use force in self-defense; military aggression is invariably defended as self-defense. However, we do not use this as a rule against allowing states the right to go to war in self-defense, so why should we treat the case of intervention differently?

Lastly, it may be said that allowing interventions would destroy state sovereignty, and that state sovereignty is the only protection that smaller states have against the tyranny of larger states.[34]

As is perhaps obvious, I do not think that we should take it without argument that the idea of the sovereignty of states has been a great success in recent world history. Nor is it clear that the fact of state sovereignty could not co-exist with a less restrictive rule on intervention. The argument in any case is flawed. It assumes that, if we had a more complex and less restrictive rule on intervention, states would abuse it. However, if we assume that larger states will routinely abuse international law, then smaller states have no protection against their tyranny anyway and had better simply find alliances with larger ones. Either states will obey international law or they will not; if they will, then it matters that we get the rules right; if they will not, then it does not matter what the rules are.

Conclusion

We may conclude by returning to the dispute about the Falklands. I think the UK's armed resistance may well have been justified. The invasion was, I think, illegal, and in the absence of an international body effectively able to enforce international law, the UK had a right, and perhaps a duty, to resist it if it could be successfully resisted at a proportional cost. Whether the cost was a proportional one is perhaps a complicated matter, depending on how important one thinks is the establishment of the rule of international law and what the results would have been of alternative courses of action. I do not, however, think it was justified merely because the inhabitants preferred to be ruled by the UK rather than by Argentina; that was, in their case, a valid preference, but it was not worth the lives that it cost to realize it. If it had been justified on such a ground, then I think that an armed intervention would also have been justified in the fictitious scenario that I imagined (though, under the existing scheme of things that would have been illegal, and as long as that were true that would be a reason against it).

My argument, then, has not been in favor of military interventions, though I think that an acceptable rule in international law would be less restrictive than what is generally accepted today. I think that *armed* intervention is very rarely justified, but that is not because it is intervention, but because it is armed, and I think that the use of armed force is very rarely justified, even in self-defense, whether in revolution, war, or intervention. On the other hand, other sorts of intervention, such as covert action or sanctions, are more easily justified than is sometimes thought. In short, our concern should be less with who mounts resistance to a government, and rather more with why, and how, it is mounted.

Obviously, this conclusion sits most easily with a generally individualist and cosmopolitan outlook. It also sits most easily with such an outlook to think that the appropriate agency for intervention ought normally to be the UN, just as the proper agency for armed intervention in domestic politics is normally the police force. This, however, would require considerable change in the UN.

For one thing, the veto power possessed by members of the security council is, of course, a major problem, and one which is unlikely to be solved in the near future (since each member has a veto power over proposals about the veto power). And, since the use of military action cannot be entirely ruled out the UN would need to be given a proper armed force.[35] There has been a little progress on this, but there are, as yet, few grounds for serious optimism. In the absence of an effective UN, the burden must fall elsewhere. Regional groupings such as the European Union and North Atlantic Treaty Organization have, it seems to me, greater moral standing than the neighbor states that have in fact carried out most interventions. On the other hand, those neighboring states are, at the present time, often likely to intervene more effectively than regional groupings, and, when there is a need to intervene, it is on them that the duty will often fall.

Notes

1. "Since international law recognizes the right of revolution, it cannot permit other states to intervene to prevent it," Quincy Wright, "Subversive Intervention," *American Journal of International Law* 54 (1960): 521-35, at 529. Stuart Harris, *Cases and Materials on International Law*, 3rd ed. (London: Sweet and Maxwell, 1983) 651, remarks that this "probably represents the majority view of writers today."

2. Article 2(7) of the UN Charter says: "Nothing contained in the present Charter shall authorize the United Nations to intervene in matters which are essentially within the domestic jurisdiction of any state or shall require the Members to submit such matters to settlement under the present Charter..."

General Assembly Resolution 2131 (XX), § 1 (1966) says: "No state has the right to intervene, directly or indirectly, for any reason whatever, in the internal or external affairs of any other state. Consequently, armed intervention and all other forms of interference or attempted threats against the personality of the state or against its political, economic and cultural elements, are condemned."

The legal position may not be quite as clear as these ringing terms may suggest. Article 2(7) "does not apply if the United Nations agency is of the opinion that a breach of a specific legal obligation relating to human rights in the Charter has occurred. In practice, organs of the United Nations have further reduced the effect of the reservation, by construing certain provisions relating to human rights, which might seem only hortatory, as presenting definite and active legal obligations." Ian Brownlie, *Principles of Public International Law*, 5th ed. (Oxford: Clarendon Press, 1998) 558. See also Geoffrey Best, *War and Law Since 1945* (Oxford: Clarendon Press, 1994) 58.

The use of force against a sovereign state is generally recognized to be morally legitimate in (1) self-defense and (2) counter-intervention. There is some dispute about (3) the use of force to protect one's own nationals. Many accept (4) the use of humanitarian intervention in cases of gross violations of human rights, such as genocide and mass enslavement; few accept humanitarian intervention in cases less than this.

3. There may be some sense in which rational argument is coercive, but in moral and legal contexts it is obviously important to mark a distinction here.

4. Arend and Beck suggest this; see, Anthony Clark Arend and Robert J. Beck, *International Law and the Use of Force: Beyond the UN Charter Paradigm* (London: Routledge, 1993) 94; Murphy says that the motive must be *primarily* humanitarian; see, Sean D. Murphy, *Humanitarian Intervention. The United Nations in an Evolving World Order* (Philadelphia, PA: University of Pennsylvania Press, 1996) 15.

5. We shall leave aside the problem that it is not unproblematic to speak of a nation's motives. Are we speaking of the motives of the politicians, the people at large, those responsible for the decision ...?

6. It may become relevant when the motive alters the nature of the action, as in, perhaps, racially motivated crimes.

7. "International law has no alternative but to accept war, independently of the justice of its origin, as a relation which the parties to it may set up if they choose, and to busy itself only in regulating the effects of the relation"; W.E. Hall, ed., *A Treatise on International Law*, 8th ed. (Oxford: Oxford University Press, 1924) 82.

8. The Pact of Paris condemned "recourse to war for the solution of international controversies" and signatories renounced it "as an instrument of national policy." It was not generally taken as prohibiting war in self-defense. Article 2(4) of the UN Charter restricts nations in the "threat or use of force," but 51 specifically allows for the use of armed force in self-defense, though with some UN oversight. The substance of Article 2(4) was subsequently elaborated in the General Assembly Resolution 2625 (XXV), October 24, 1970 (Declaration on Principles of International Law concerning Friendly Relations and Co-operation among States in Accordance with the Charter of the United Nations).

9. The matter is, of course, somewhat complicated in reality.

10. Article 52 of the UN Charter implies that forceful self-defense must be suspended once the UN has "taken measures necessary to maintain international peace and security," and Argentina argued that by the time the UK responded this had happened. But this referred only to Security Council resolution 502, which demanded that hostilities should cease, Argentina should withdraw her forces, and that negotiations should take place; that demand, which in any case was not acceded to by Argentina, by itself could hardly be thought to be a measure necessary to maintain international peace and security.

11. The UK government attached considerable weight to the fact that the UK had peacefully administered the islands since 1833; this — in itself — provides no moral justification, though it connects with the two possible justifications I discuss.

12. "An armed attack by one state upon another in furtherance of the principle of self-determination is not permitted, despite the emphasis placed upon that principle in recent years." Harris 643.

13. For the other one-tenth, see Brownlie 289ff.

14. Michael Walzer, "Humanitarian Intervention Reconsidered," *Dissent* (2002, forthcoming).

15. Michael Walzer, "The Moral Standing of States: A Response to Four Critics," *Philosophy and Public Affairs* 9 (1980): 209-29. Walzer's position here is slightly different from that put forward in his *Just and Unjust Wars* (New York: Basic Books, 1977) Ch. 6.

16. Walzer, "The Moral Standing of States" 212.

17. Walzer, "The Moral Standing of States" 214.

18. Walzer, "The Moral Standing of States " 212.

19. Walzer, "The Moral Standing of States" 225.

20. Walzer, "The Moral Standing of States" 214.

21. Walzer, "The Moral Standing of States" 220ff.

22. For a careful account of Hohfeld's scheme of rights, see Judith Jarvis Thomson, *The Realm of Rights* (Cambridge, MA: Harvard University Press, 1990) Ch. 1.

23. You may not be required to risk your life to save another who, without your aid, will certainly die. It does not follow from this that a third person may not also risk your life if the alternative is that someone else will certainly die.

24. Walzer, "The Moral Standing of States" 212.

25. Our "conduct, in the first instance at least, cannot be determined by either knowledge or judgment. It is, or ought to be, determined instead by a morally necessary presumption: that there exists a certain 'fit' between the community and its government, and that the state is 'legitimate'" (Walzer, "The Moral Standing of States" 212).

26. Walzer, "The Moral Standing of States" 212. Again: we should have "respect for communal integrity and for different patterns of cultural and political development" (215f.).

27. Walzer, "The Moral Standing of States" 226.

28. If processes have value, then processes that maximize the occurrence of those processes should be promoted, and this can be counter-intuitive.

29. But I wonder what would have happened if the UK had intervened in Sierra Leone in 1964 when the country became a dictatorship? (Not so long ago, the peace was effectively kept in that state for two years by a couple of hundred South African mercenaries.)

30. Walzer, "The Moral Standing of States" 226.

31. Groups can, of course, have *legal* rights which are not reducible in this way.

32. Though, it is not easy to know what the course of things would have been in Somalia if the US had remained instead of pulling out after the debacle in Mogadishu.

33. The invasion was followed by about ten years of considerable unrest in which a large number of people lost their lives. The problems are, of course, not yet over. But it seems fair to assume that the situation would have been yet more awful without Tanzania's involvement.

34. Cf. Caroline Thomas, "The Pragmatic Case Against Intervention," *Political Theory, International Relations, and the Ethics of Intervention*, ed. Ian Forbes and Mark Hoffmann (London: St. Martin's Press, 1993) 95.

35. See Boutros Boutros-Ghali, *An Agenda for Peace*, §§43—45 (United Nations, 1992). Boutros-Ghali correctly emphasizes the potential deterrent effectiveness of such a force.

On the general question of reforming the UN, see E. Childers, "UN Mechanisms and Capacities for Intervention," *The Challenge to Intervene: A New Role for the United Nations?*, ed. E. Ferris (Uppsala, Sweden: Life and Peace Institute, 1992); and E. Childers and B. Urquhart, *Renewing the United Nations System* (Uppsala, Sweden: Hammerskjöld Foundation, 1994).

2

Humanitarian Intervention: Some Doubts

Burleigh Wilkins

If Locke was correct, and I think he was, revolution is justified when there is systematic violation of the rights to life, liberty, and property with no peaceful redress in sight. I believe that secession and even terrorism are also justified when these conditions obtain. But what about humanitarian intervention? Is it also justified in such a situation? Many of us hesitate when confronted by this question, but why? Is it because humanitarian intervention involves military action by some state or states against another state? Is it because it may raise questions about the legitimacy of a state's sovereignty, questions which even the most secure liberal democracy may feel uncomfortable in addressing? Are even more egregious violations of human rights required in the case of humanitarian intervention than in the cases of revolution, secession, and terrorism? Of course, attempted justifications of humanitarian intervention may focus upon issues other than human rights violations, such as the need to establish or reestablish a democracy or to put an end to a vicious civil war, but these issues, although separate from the issue of human rights violations, may nevertheless be related to it. For purposes of this chapter, I shall be concerned only with human rights violations as a possible ground for humanitarian intervention.

Although it involves the violation of a state's independence and territorial integrity, humanitarian intervention is usually distinguished from war on the ground that the loss of independence and territorial integrity is limited in time and scope. Also it is regarded as a means and not an end, with the end being not conquest or the acquisition of land but the restoration or establishment of protection for basic human rights. But how long before a temporary incursion becomes an occupation? And does not the protection of human rights necessitate at times a change of government, as part of what is sometimes called "a comprehensive settlement"? And what, if anything, can the intervening power(s) do about the culture or way of life which may underlie a government's violation of human rights?

International law seems committed to respect for the sovereignty of states, to the protection of human rights, and to the maintenance of peaceful relations among states. In an ideal world where, say, all states are liberal democracies, all three of these commitments would presumably be honored. There is Michael Doyle's "law" that no democracies ever fight one another, but is this a law or just a trend? In any event, in the real world it may be impossible to provide equal protection for sovereignty, human rights, and peaceful co-existence among states. Here we can note the temptation to treat human rights violations in one state as a threat to the peace and security of all states, or at least of neighboring states, and to use this as a justification for the violation of a nation's sovereignty, although this may in some cases seem farfetched and even disingenuous.

Perhaps humanitarian intervention isn't war, but is it enough like war that the doctrine of just war—with its requirements that a war be fought for a just cause and in a just manner, with an expectation of success, and with a respect for proportionality between the means being employed and the end being sought—can be applied? Would a little fine-tuning help? Justice can be cashed in terms of human rights, with the stipulation that the intervention will not become an all-out war and that it will not last too long. *Jus ad interventionem*. It has a fine ring to it! And the numbers are simply appalling: four times as many deaths in the twentieth century at the hands of the victims' own government or as a result of civil strife than from all the wars between states.[1]

Is the model of Good Samaritan intervention by an individual person(s) to assist an individual under attack by another at all helpful here? But these interventions, in those jurisdictions where they are legally mandated, are called for only in cases where the convenience and not the lives of third-party interveners is at risk. Here the law seems to follow common morality: if an individual chooses to risk his or her life to come to the aid of another, this is not considered a duty but a supererogatory act. Does this help explain the cautious manner in which political philosophers speak only of a right of intervention and the silence of philosophers such as Walzer and Rawls on whether humanitarian intervention may be a duty?[2] Make no mistake: humanitarian intervention involves a high probability that the intervening party will take casualties. Sometimes the mere presence of troops may lead to casualties, as "mission creep" is a fact of geopolitical life. This is what happened in Somalia where American troops who were initially dispatched to protect humanitarian aid supplies for a starving populace got caught in a struggle between rival warlords.

However, consider the case where an intervening party takes no casualties, as for example the US-NATO intervention in Kosovo which relied entirely upon high altitude bombings to achieve its objectives. This kind of attack, which critics have likened to shooting fish in a barrel, raises fundamental questions of fairness in how an intervention is conducted.

Might not humanitarian intervention sometimes yield just the opposite effect where the protection of human rights is concerned? There are two real possibilities. An oppressive government may be prompted to become even more oppressive in response to an intervention, with confidence that its supporters and even some of its previous critics will "rally round the flag." Or, once intervention occurs, the leadership of an opposition group may become more militant and disrespectful of the rights of others, or the leadership may pass into the hands of a more militant faction with even less respect for human rights than the oppressive regime with which we started out.

Almost everyone agrees that humanitarian intervention might be justified in some cases, but real world examples may prove troublesome. Take the example of the persecution of Jews in Nazi Germany. When would humanitarian intervention have been justified? Before or after *Kristallnacht*? Or only after the Holocaust had begun? By then the West was already at war with Germany for other reasons. What this example shows is the difficulty in pointing to the time when intervention would have become justified, and the certainty that early intervention would have inevitably escalated into an all-out war that the West was not prepared, militarily or psychologically, to fight. The same is true today when we raise the question of what to do about Tibet or Chechnya. The answer is that we can do very little with powers that have nuclear weapons at their disposal. And, of course, we would not pressure allies such as Turkey over its mistreatment of the Kurds as much as we would pressure non-allies over less severe mistreatment of some of their citizens.

Michael J. Smith in a defense of humanitarian intervention candidly admits that there "simply won't be consistency" in our reactions to human rights violations, but he asks, "Is it more ethical to say that, since I cannot do everything everywhere consistently, I should do nothing?"[3] Smith proposes that we adopt a scale of evil where human rights abuses are concerned; on this scale Virginia's frequent use of the death penalty would rank far below the massacres in Rwanda and Cambodia since "few disinterested observers would urge or welcome the forcible landing of an international military force to prevent Virginia's next execution." Smith seems to believe that there is nothing problematic about how rankings on a scale of evil would be determined. This might be true if the executions in Virginia and the massacres in Rwanda and Cambodia were placed at opposite ends of the scale, but other cases might prove more difficult to rank.

There are, as Smith points out, a few success stories for humanitarian intervention, such as India's intervention in East Pakistan and Tanzania's intervention in Uganda. But India's role in the liberation of Bangladesh, according to some observers, only made matters worse, and, given the history of India-Pakistan relations, it may be that India's intervention was not driven mainly by humanitarian concerns. This leaves us with Tanzania's overthrow of the monstrous Idi Amin in Uganda. Such a small success can hardly lend much support to the principle of humanitarian intervention, and large successes are not to be expected. Undoubtedly, as Smith reminds us, there are moral evils far greater than inconsistency, and to do nothing in the face of evil may well be one of them. It is not, however, the problem of consistency per se that concerns me but the problem of how targets for humanitarian intervention get selected.

Scholars agree that there are no instances of purely humanitarian intervention, and, given what we know about the complexity of human motivation and of the relations among states, this is scarcely surprising. Of course, some cases of allegedly humanitarian intervention are clearly bogus, e.g., Hitler's invasion of Czechoslovakia on the ground of protecting the human rights of the German minority. We all know that for Hitler human rights stopped with German rights, but other cases are more subtle. Sometimes humanitarian intervention may be used in part to settle old grudges, as was alleged against Boutros Boutros-Ghali where Somalia was concerned, or humanitarian intervention may be used against states which have previously fallen upon disfavor in our eyes. Serbia needs to be taught a lesson, as the American Secretary of State put it during the US-NATO intervention in Kosovo. Intervention may also be used in restoring a state's moral standing in the eyes of others. For example, American intervention in Bosnia was undoubtedly influenced by the desire to overcome anti-American sentiments in the Muslim world arising from the Gulf War and to restore the American "reputation" for fairness and evenhandedness. One thing we can be sure of is that humanitarian intervention will not occur if there is a risk of a major conflict in which the intervening power(s) can be expected to take significant casualties. It may be possible to devise a scale of evil, as Smith believes, but there already is a scale of power, and no one seriously believes that evils of great magnitude will trump considerations of relative power.

Because of my doubts about humanitarian intervention I shall not explore in any detail the crucial question of who might best decide whether humanitarian intervention is warranted and who should carry out the intervention. Unilateral intervention by a single state has the advantage of swiftness but runs the risk of partiality and of appearing to be a species of "gunboat diplomacy." Regional organizations should be better at filtering out biases, but they may be dominated by a single great power. The UN may take too long in its decision-making, but it is less likely to be biased and has enjoyed, at least until recently, great moral stature. The UN seems to be the best organization for making a decision about intervention, but the problem of consensus is troubling. Kofi Annan in his report on the tragedy of Srebrenica took responsibility for the UN and the part it played. But politicians and bureaucrats are adroit at taking responsibility in such a way as to shift responsibility. In the "lessons" to be learned from the tragedy, Annan ranked the lack of a common "political will" high on his list of causes which will need to be addressed to avoid future Srebrenicas.[4] However, the lack of a common political will has not been present in all of the activities of the UN as, for example, in the Gulf War which turned on the conquest of one state by another. In cases where there is no common political will, is doing nothing not preferable to the kind of bungling which contributes to disasters like Srebrenica?

The lack of a common political will is, of course, not necessarily confined to the international arena. Domestic support in a state for humanitarian intervention may ebb and flow, depending on the strength of opposed political parties and upon their commitment to a particular humanitarian intervention. One concern I have is the following: once it has been decided that humanitarian intervention is warranted in a particular situation, crucial steps that a more patient diplomacy might pursue may be skipped. An example of this is the haste with which the US and NATO decided to attack Serbia before negotiations were given a real chance—negotiations which were, in fact, a form of ultimatum. There is also the danger of self-righteousness which may lead the UN or other state to make demands which no self-respecting state could possibly accept, such as permitting foreign troops to travel at will throughout its territory or the holding of a plebiscite concerning independence for a contested region.

The current international situation can be characterized as follows. Friends and foes alike are nervous over the US-NATO intervention in Kosovo. How long will troops continue to be deployed there? What will count as a successful termination of the mission? Does it set a precedent for future interventions elsewhere in the name of human rights? Whatever happened to the duty of non-intervention, and what kind of duty is it anyway?

One possible reading of the duty of non-intervention is that it is an absolute duty, and various UN agreements including the Charter appear to support this interpretation. However, many moral philosophers would deny that a duty—or a right—can be absolute, that is, obtaining under all circumstances. Perhaps we should try to move in one of two other directions. We could say that the duty of non-intervention is *prima facie*, that is, that there is a strong presumption against intervention but one that can be overridden when there are compelling reasons to do so. Or we could try to write out a list of exceptions and make this list an explicit part of the formulation of the duty of non-intervention. What are some of these exceptions? Cases where we are invited to intervene by the legitimate government of a state? Cases where we can prevent or suppress systematic violations of human rights? Cases where we can assist in struggles for "national liberation"? But, except for the case where the intervention is invited, all other cases will be controversial and will call for further elaboration or refinement. The question still remains of whether these elaborations and refinements would be stated as explicit parts of the duty of non-intervention. For various reasons the project of a definitive list of exceptions to any duty—including that of non-intervention—seems doomed to failure. Seeing the duty of non-intervention as *prima facie* becomes a more attractive alternative if only by default. However, it might still be argued that the duty of non-intervention is absolute and that we only need add "except in the case of an emergency." All deontological rules, it is sometimes argued, are properly construed in this way, and the emergency exception would be difficult to satisfy. This may be part of the problem: although some non-emergency but justifiable reasons for intervention may be compelling, one person's emergency may be another person's difficulty which can be resolved short of intervention.

A final possibility is an openly purposive or teleological reading of the duty of non-intervention: it is to be respected except when intervention serves an end or purpose deemed morally justifiable, in accordance with, for example, utilitarianism or Marxism. However, where international law is concerned this purposive or teleological reading of the duty of non-intervention would strain the associative model of the UN and other forms of cooperation among states, as described by Terry Nardin.[5] What is to prevent the protection and especially the promotion of human rights from becoming as divisive as any other teleological reading of the duty of non-intervention? The protection and promotion of human rights might be divisive not only between states that champion human rights and those that do not, but also among states that support human rights but fail to agree on the appropriateness of particular interventions. Consider, for example, the controversies surrounding the Reagan administration's policies in Nicaragua and especially that administration's refusal to acknowledge that the American bombing of Nicaragua's harbors fell under the jurisdiction of the International Court of Justice.

I admit to having grown weary, or at least wary, of disjunctions between doing something and doing nothing. In the present case there are many things which can be done to advance the cause of human rights which fall short of humanitarian intervention. One way to ameliorate conflicts between liberal and decent societies on the one hand and outlaw states on the other is, simply put, trade. There is Thomas Friedman's "law" that no two countries with MacDonalds have ever gone to war with one another. Where human rights issues are concerned the strategy, which sounds simple in the abstract, is to link trading privileges with the acceptance of human rights covenants, as, for example, was the case with the European Council when it granted trading privileges to Russia. In the eighteenth century, the Chinese Emperor wrote to the emissary of King George III that he did not wish to trade with the British since the Chinese had no interest in Britain's clever gadgets. Fortunately for us, and the prospects of a stable world order, all the world seems mad to have the US's clever gadgets. The question of how to take this market for American goods and use it to promote the cause of human rights is, however, a question of statecraft to which, as a philosopher, I have nothing to contribute beyond counsels of prudence. However, in the remainder of this paper I shall explore some conceptual matters which may help clarify the connections between morality and international law.

One possible way to approach this problem is to underscore the moral content of international law and to see it as being in itself an ethical tradition. Of course, this interpretation of international law runs counter to the "realist" school of thought, which reduces all relations among states to questions of national interest. Treaties are made to be broken, according to the realist, whenever one side sees an advantage in doing so, and states are expected to spy not only upon their enemies but upon their friends as well. Trust no one, and promote national self-interest by whatever means are judged to be necessary. Against this bleak picture of the relations among states, which, of course, is not entirely mistaken, it is possible to think of international law as an ethical tradition in its own right similar to natural law theory, Kantianism, utilitarianism, Marxism, etc. This is Terry Nardin's position: ethical traditions evolve over time, and they involve judgments about the application of principles to particular situations.[6] Certainly Nardin is right, since one would be hard pressed to articulate a sharp distinction between legal and moral principles and the ways in which they are applied to particular cases. In what follows, however, I shall be concerned with international law not as an ethical tradition but with the moral obligations to which it gives rise where the conduct of states is concerned.

I begin this final portion of my paper with a confession about international law. I find it to be a perplexing mixture of treaties among states, customary practices among states, the charters and instruments of the United Nations and several regional organizations, the decisions of various international tribunals, and even the writings of international lawyers. International law is so complex and in such a state of change that it cannot, according to some scholars, readily be codified. Then, of course, there is the problem of sanctions or enforcement, a problem so important some commentators have concluded that, strictly speaking, international law is not law at all. Thus, there is something very tentative in what I say when I speak of international law as a legal system.

A municipal legal system differs from mere orders and commands in that it imposes moral duties and obligations upon all members of a society, and there is a general recognition, not limited to legal philosophers, that there is a moral obligation to obey all the laws of a municipal legal system. You cannot pick and choose which laws you will obey. Transposing this picture to international law results in the following: all states are morally bound to respect the provisions of international law, just as individuals are morally bound to respect the provisions of municipal law. But are states the kinds of things that can have moral duties and obligations? Why not, provided we see them as organized groups of individuals bound together by common rules? At the very least it is coherent to say that organized groups of individuals can undertake or enter into agreements with other organized groups of individuals. In fact, this seems to be what actually happens on a daily basis where, for example, the transactions of business corporations are concerned. Where international law is concerned, the agreements between organized groups can be understood in terms of treaties and even customary practices among states.

It is noteworthy that the principles governing the relations among peoples which we find in John Rawls's *The Law of Peoples* are themselves taken from international law. According to Rawls, these principles are: peoples are to observe a duty of non-intervention, peoples are to honor human rights, peoples are to observe treaties and undertakings, and peoples are equal and are parties to the agreements that bind them. Rawls writes that "These familiar and largely traditional principles I take from the history and usage of international law and practice. The parties are not given a menu of alternative principles and ideals from which to select, as they are in *Political Liberalism* or in *A Theory of Justice*. Rather, the representatives of well-ordered peoples simply reflect on the advantages of these principles of equality among peoples and see no reason to depart from them or to propose alternatives."[7] In Rawls's second Original Position, the representatives of liberal and decent hierarchical peoples select principles that are binding upon all peoples, including outlaw states. (Could there ever be an outlaw people for Rawls? Perhaps not, given, for example, the careful way in which he tries to distinguish the Nazi state from the German people. Here he disagrees with David Goldhagen's position in *Hitler's Willing Executioners*. The possibility that a coercive demonic political leadership could in time produce a demonic people merits careful consideration.)[8] If I am correct, both Rawls's account of the principles governing the relations of peoples and international law as *it already is* presuppose the idea of international law conceived of as a legal system.

The duty of non-intervention is on my interpretation a moral duty binding upon all states, and it is one of many such duties. Here we should note once more the importance of our conceiving of international law as a legal system.

It would be nonsensical to speak of a moral obligation to obey a single principle or to abide by a single agreement standing in isolation from a system of principles or agreements. (There is an analog here, I think, with science where scientific laws are seen as part of a system.) All states are morally bound not to intervene in the domestic affairs of other states. Of course all states are also bound to respect human rights; this would be especially true of the member states of the UN and even more so of those states which have signed the two UN Human Rights Covenants. However there are no provisions in the UN Charter or in these covenants for humanitarian intervention in the domestic affairs of states that do not respect human rights. In the past any such intervention clearly would have been illegal, but now things seem less certain. Perhaps in some circumstances humanitarian intervention may trump the obligation of states not to interfere in the domestic affairs of other states. In this connection it is regrettable, though understandable, that the International Court of Justice refused to rule on the legality of US-NATO intervention in Kosovo. At the risk of sounding like a democratic populist in international law when I am emphatically not a democratic populist where American domestic law is concerned, I think humanitarian intervention gives rise to such complex issues that it should be referred to the legislature. Let the member states of the UN address directly the question of whether humanitarian intervention is permissible, and if need be let us amend the Charter. Let us vote humanitarian intervention up or down, but let us not leave it to be decided on a case-by-case basis. Law, ideally, should satisfy the requirements of justice, but at the very least states no less than individuals need to know what the legal consequences of certain courses of conduct may be.[9]

I want to conclude on a cautiously optimistic note, which I think is consistent with the interpretation of international law as a legal system. According to *Political Liberalism*,[10] John Rawls's history of how the West evolved in a liberal and tolerant direction, two variables were highlighted as important. First was luck, and second was a growing appreciation on the part of individuals with different belief systems of the mutual advantages arising from limited *modus vivendi* agreements. From this it was a short step, historically speaking, to the moral quest for fair rules of social cooperation. Where relations among states are concerned, the world today has an additional advantage in international law, conceived of as a legal system that gives rise to moral obligations among states. However the question of humanitarian intervention is resolved, whether or not it is seen as a right or even as a duty, all states—not just liberal or decent states—are under an obligation to abide by international law.

43

Notes

1. See Sean O. Murphy, *Humanitarian Intervention* (Philadelphia: University of Pennsylvania Press, 1996).

2. Michael Walzer, *Just and Unjust Wars* (New York: Basic Books, 1997). John Rawls, *The Law of Peoples* (Cambridge, MA: Harvard University Press, 1999) 81, 93-94n. Stanley Hoffmann in *The Ethics and Politics of Intervention* (Notre Dame, IN: University of Notre Dame Press, 1996) 12-39, claims that he is more Kantian than Rawls because he believes there is a duty of intervention, but both are more Kantian than Kant who did not believe in intervention.

3. Michael J. Smith, "Humanitarian Intervention: An Overview of the Ethical Issues," *Ethics and International Affairs* 12 (1998): 78.

4. Report of the Secretary General Pursuant to General Assembly Resolution 53/35 (1998).

5. Terry Nardin, *Law, Morality, and the Relations of States* (Princeton, NJ: Princeton University Press, 1983).

6. Terry Nardin, "Ethical Traditions in International Affairs," *Traditions of International Ethics*, ed. Terry Nardin and David R. Mapels (Cambridge: Cambridge University Press, 1992) 1-23.

7. Rawls 41.

8. Rawls 100-01n.

9. Anthony Ellis thinks the small states in the UN would probably defeat any amendment permitting humanitarian intervention. I am not sure this is so, but, if it is, this would reflect a failure by the UN to respect the moral equality of all member states, a failure which could perhaps be alleviated by other changes in the way the UN operates, for example, by changes in the veto powers of the permanent members of the Security Council.

10. John Rawls, *Political Liberalism* (New York: Columbia University Press, 1993).

3

Foreign Armed Intervention: Between Justified Aid and Illegal Violence

Jovan Babic

Grounds for Intervention

Intervention in the affairs of other states or nations is not a novel fact of social life. Events in foreign countries, particularly if they involve great suffering, can hardly remain simply an internal matter. Many intra-state concerns and interests, not just national security, are importantly affected by external developments, perhaps just as much or more than by internal ones. In recent times, however, a new idiom as a way of reflecting on these facts has become prevalent. The phrase in question is "humanitarian intervention." Contrary to what one might readily suppose, however, the phrase does not stand for some rescue operation,[1] such as may be undertaken in the case of earthquakes, major floods, or catastrophic levels of poverty, despair, and famine. Instead, the term refers to a military operation in a foreign country with alleged humanitarian rationale. On this count, the phrase-component "intervention" takes semantic precedence in its contribution to the full meaning of the phrase over the word "humanitarian." The specific role of the latter phrase-component is to indicate that a justified and acceptable form of military operation is in question, rather than one that is unjustified and unacceptable. This is in keeping with the fact that the word "intervention" takes the primary semantic role in the complete phrase, while the word "humanitarian" has the role of the attribute, modifying the main term.

Furthermore, this newly fashioned use of the term "humanitarian" purports to indicate that the intervention so designated takes as its purpose and source of justification the protection, defense, or restitution of those items specifically referred to by the term "human rights." This is in contrast to interventions that might not be so designated. The term "humanitarian" is used in a way that characterizes the related justification for action as uniquely

45

valid and universal. As a device to express a new ideology or primary political dogma, it appears to single out a set standard applicable to all valid forms of political governance anywhere on the globe.

Previously, the language was different, while often the actions were much the same. Interventions were accompanied by their own vocabulary and by an articulation of justifying reasons describing their necessity. A justification has always been a component part of any military intervention. Recall Korea, Hungary, Vietnam, Czechoslovakia, and Afghanistan in the 1980s. All these earlier cases of intervention—prior to the era of "humanitarian intervention"—offered "defense" as their justification. They differed only with respect to what was defended. Consequently, the earlier practice made room for heterogeneity of values that could be legitimately "defended" in this way. By contrast, the current trend is toward an unvarying "justification" of intervention in terms of human rights. Protection of human rights is taken to represent the set of values that forms the basis for constituting rules of conduct, and those rules must be obeyed universally because those values are taken to be universal. As such, they are not only to be defended, but imposed as well.

The question of whether or not there are any truly universal values in the world is a very difficult one. Equally complex is the related question of how and on what grounds some items are taken as representing universal values. Though certainly important, these matters are well beyond the scope of the present study. We shall instead narrow our attention to the legal realm and framework of possible justification of intervention. Specifically, the issue that will concern us is whether it is possible to regulate the practice of humanitarian intervention so that it would be legal or illegal according to some previously specified conditions. To be precise, the attention will be on whether or not the emphasis on "human rights" can furnish the requisite universal-value foundation for such justification. Certainly, some values we are dealing with are universal by their very nature. These are *moral* values—for example, those embodied in the concept of (self-)defense. Others, presumably, are not universal, such as, among others, *political* values—for example, those embodied in the concept of the "right to self-determination." In the human rights ideology, however, no room exists for distinctions of this sort, for it assumes that *all* values from some set (as yet not adequately defined) are universal and binding.

This presumption that "human rights" represent some set of universal values in fact indicates their specific ideological purpose: to create an atmosphere of self-evidence. In this context, self-evidence assumes the place of explication; that is, the process of offering (sufficiently) good reasons for humanitarian intervention (in some concrete case) proves redundant. The appeal to self-evidence—a form of reasonless (gratuitous) acceptance—is by no means a novel scheme of political justification. As with doctrines based on divine revelation or validated by a sacred book, self-evidence functions as a form of reductionism absorbing all reasons from a list supplied in advance. Additionally, it is assumed by the indoctrinated that this list is well defined and complete. This explains a sort of nervousness among "believers" when what is taken to be obvious is put in question or when reasons for it are demanded, for all the reasons have already been given in advance, and any reasoning may require only a simple deduction.

Prior procedures for justifying armed intervention exhibited the same structure, relying heavily on the mechanism of self-evidence. What is novel with appeals to "humanitarian" interventions is that the argument offered for codifying the right of intervention within international law exhibits hitherto nonexistent uniformity. The previous era's justifying reasons for intervention, given in terms of a "defense" of some value—rather than its "protection" or "promotion"—always enjoyed a certain heterogeneity, in that the values that were defended did not require prior definition as universal values. Instead, the defense of a given value was a matter of law and was justified on a legal basis. This was not the case only when a party defended itself, but also in the instances assistance was offered to the parties requesting such help based on an already well-defined right to self-defense. These were almost always legal governments experiencing some form of attack (internal or external). Unable to secure protection on their own, they sought outside help (e.g., South Vietnam or Afghanistan). However, different reasons might have been operative as well—for example, the violation, or perceived violation, of some previously agreed-upon obligations that were deemed so binding that their violation could serve as a sufficient justifying reason for intervention. (An example of this sort might be Czechoslovakia's attempt to abolish the "binding orthodox path of socialist development" in 1968.) In any case, up until very recently the cases of purportedly justified foreign armed interventions were not designed to defend (or one might better say, to promote and protect) some uniformly defined and invariable value.

A characteristic feature of our world, however, is its heterogeneity of accepted values. Hence, the universalistic position defined in terms of the presumption that some specific set of values is universally valid proves inadequate. If this stance, so appropriate in morality, were allowed in politics, a sort of uniformity in the world would be produced, threatening the plurality of cultural and civilizational patterns that have served many people and their collectives as the basis for constructing the meaning of their existence. In any event, even to those who impose their civilizational matrix or their ideology onto others, this matrix or ideology represents the basis for constructing their own life projects and gives meaning to their lives. Sometimes the experience of identifying with a particular ideology is so intense that people are willing to spread their value matrix worldwide, often in the form of crusade-like fanaticism. Having respect for others, however, presupposes that they are free to articulate their own *Weltanschauung* in their own way, maybe even in quite a different way. So, assuming that respect for others is definitionally connected with the moral criterion, it seems that morality, being itself universal, requires not only the possibility of heterogeneity, but also its real presence in the world.

In order to provide protection for this heterogeneity in the world any community of states must adhere to the rule that all states are in principle equals. This is the source of the right states have to freely arrange for themselves their internal affairs in accordance with their own traditions and histories. The restriction, of course, implies that this freedom must be harmonized with the freedom of other such political communities, allowing them to do the same. Insistence on a uniform model of social and political life threatens both this heterogeneity and the possibility of political freedom. In order to avoid this danger, a set of very strong restrictions must be placed on interference in the internal affairs of other states. These boundaries must at the least be such that, with regard to the distinction between intervention and interference, they principally preclude the latter and then establish clear rules or restrictions on the former. All of this, of course, is covered very well in various conventions of international organizations (the UN and others) and in existing international law.

This may seem deficient to those who reject any distinction between law and morality, who think a right which is not clearly morally justified is not legally grounded either. This position requires that in law, too, we must have a universally uniform decision-making process to determine what is right and what is not. In morality, as already mentioned, we have (or at least I am inclined to think we have) a universal criterion of evaluation, and its application in all situations should lead everyone to the same assessment. But in political matters, after all, things stand differently. Political questions deal with what human collectives articulate as their important and primary interests. These become community interests because of the value the group attaches to them. Consequently, they require special protection by means of rules that obligate all to respect them—on pain of sanctions—though those rules (even when legally articulated) are not or need not (and even cannot) be universal. Legal norms or laws lack universality. Their validity is bound instead by territory, just as their content is limited to the expression of a particular collective *want* albeit in some general way, i.e., collective legislative *will*. Laws give expression to what is *wanted* to be the case, rather than what *ought* to be so. Legal norms are to a much greater degree than moral norms an expression of human freedom and the related need that it not only be *restricted* (as in morality) but also *guaranteed* (by laws). These norms in fact express the constitutive or vital interests of some specific nation, a state, in essentially the same way political interests are articulated within some state, though they enjoy greater generality and aspiration to durability.

Those interests may be diverse and have varied degrees of generality. For example, the interest in achieving self-determination—which could become the grounds for foreign intervention—may constitute itself in many different ways. If the sincerity of a desire to secede were the determining criterion of legitimacy regarding a secessionist claim (just as such sincerity is a necessary condition of legitimacy of other democratically expressed forms of collective will), we could never discern fully justified cases from those that are less so. It is perfectly clear, however, that not all such desires, and interests based on them, are equally justified. Nor is it the case from the perspective of third-party states—whether they are disinterested or have a specific interest in the matter—that every claim to self-determination is equally compelling regarding those states' capacity to offer support and assistance. However, unless the right to self-determination is included among the (presumed) universally valid and at the same time *legally* expressible human rights, there would be no obligation for, nor a right of, other states to assist secessionists in their quest to realize this right (no matter how "pure" and plausible their justification might sound).

The Right of Intervention: Is It Also a Duty?

The "right" of intervention isn't the same as its "justification." The former concerns its legal status while the latter is concerned with the question of whether or not there is a sufficiently good reason for intervening (i.e., if it is a good means for an adopted end). Hence, an intervention might be deemed "justified" even if this meant nothing more than that there were an interest (strategic, economic, or military) that could be satisfied by this means. In this sense every intervention is per assumption justified: it would be entirely unusual that an intervention occur for no reason at all.

However, "right" could be understood here in a much more interesting way for the sake of ethical and philosophical inquiry: as a right grounded exclusively on a moral justification. In that case the nature of the relationship between the moral and legal orders will require exploration. To what extent is a moral justification as such a good or adequate basis for constituting a proper right in the legal sense? And to what degree then does this justification corroborate or nullify other kinds of justification and existing laws? However, if moral justification enjoys this kind of power, then a question must be asked about the ways of providing guarantees for its content and for its enforcement.[2]

There are arguments that clearly rely on moral reasons to account for the difficulty or impossibility of achieving a legal articulation of a right to intervention, though the issue is the formulation of a legal precept and, therefore, belongs to the domain of ethical, not legal, analysis. Roughly speaking, there are good moral reasons that require law to be constituted in a way confirmed by a certain legislative will, that restrict the domain of its validity to a given territory, and that ensure that law is not reduced to morality. These reasons provide that whatever law amounts to, it ought to be "our law," i.e., it ought to give expression to a free democratic *will* of some people who are self-governing (and not subjugated under foreign rule without its consent). An "excess of morality," particularly if this "excess" finds its expression in law, leads to the road toward fundamentalism and totalitarianism because the "replacement" of law by morality is a process that may lead to the elimination of law. This clearly would be of negative moral value. The existence of law is among the demands of morality; its existence, among other things, is dependent on resisting the reduction of law to morality. The reduction of law to morality eliminates law and seriously undermines morality, demanding the enforcement of moral rules, and hence creates a context in which the criterion of moral evaluation is enforced, in contradiction to its normal application.

Now, the term "right" refers to a notion that appears essentially vague: one implication of "having a right" is that one need not exercise it, i.e., one may freely choose to forsake it. This, however, cannot be the case with a right asserted by the phrase "the right of intervention." This right, if it is one, should not be one that could freely be forsaken, for it would not be a *prima facie* right, but a right based on a sort of exception: the prior *prima facie* prohibition of precisely the sort of action that is here claimed as a "right," i.e., the principled prohibition of intervention. Here we find an interesting dialectic: having a right to exemption from such an important prohibition implies a very strong justification to do just that. Intuitively, it seems plausible that such a right may exist only if it is at the same time also a duty.

For example, I have a right to enter into contracts, but this imposes no duty on me to do so. I am free to enter into contracts or not (or "sign on the dotted line or not,") as I please. But this right is not grounded in a (justified) exception, as would be the case with, for example, the right of intervention. This entire argument is based on the assumption that there is a difference between permission and prohibition: while no additional explication is needed in cases of permission, it is always needed in cases of prohibition. However, when a permission is parasitical on an antecedent prohibition, as in the case of the "right of intervention"—or for example the permission to kill in cases of capital punishment or self-defense (which are parasitical on an antecedent prohibition of killing)—then it is reasonable to suppose that such a permission[3] also amounts to a duty. It is not simply a right, in the sense that it is left for me to choose whether I would assert it or not in any given case. Therefore, if in some concrete case there should exist the right of intervention, then it ought to be the case that there is also a concurrent duty to intervene. Could this ever be the case, and if so under what conditions? These would be those *very rare* cases when not only a reason that may feasibly constitute a right to intervene exists, but also a concurrent duty to do so, and when this happens the right would in fact result from the coinciding duty. The right to intervene represents a duty to intervene precisely because there is an antecedent general *prima facie* duty of nonintervention. Consequently, this right cannot be a right in the usual sense affording one a (normative) choice to "exercise" it or not. This indicates that in a concrete case there might exist a compelling justifying reason for this action even though it is always *prima facie* unjustified.

Sovereignty

We live in a world made up of nation-states. While the issue of how states operate cannot be addressed here, we must focus on the aspect of their sovereignty. The world made of states cannot function without a regulative idea contained in the notion of sovereignty. This idea has two basic components. First, certification in the form of people's will is required for the validity of state law. This will[4] defines a collective that forms a state on a given territory delimited and configured by its borders. Second, the presupposition of the universal recognition of sovereignty among states makes international relations a practice that incorporates an element of following rules. A world order, consequently, is an altogether different sort of thing than the Hobbesian "state of nature" conceived as a perpetual war of each against everyone.

The regulative nature of the idea of sovereignty embodies a problem, however. On the one hand, there is the inclination toward seeing the rule contained in this idea as constitutive in nature. Otherwise, it would not be binding to a sufficient degree. On the other hand, an unlimited, absolute sovereignty is not possible. This mechanism of recognition presupposes a sort of inter-dependence, and only through the workings of this mechanism is a state perceived—and perceives itself—as a sovereign state, rather than merely an entity that aspires to that status. Mutual recognition makes possible the transition from a desire or demand for sovereignty to the status of a legitimate sovereign power. Sovereignty rests on the recognition from other members of the international community, but prior to that on the loyalty of those who are subject to the laws of that state. Hence, a double acknowledgment is required, though in different ways: the state needs both assent from those subject to the law, and recognition from other states that those laws are legitimate rather than arbitrary expressions of will in an arbitrary distribution of power.

This mechanism of recognition presupposes mutuality or reciprocity, and only through its exercise can a state become perceived—and perceive itself—as a sovereign state. It is a distinguishing factor demarcating sovereign states from entities that are merely embodying a pretension to this status (a pretension that might come in the form of a wish, a demand, etc., rather than representing a sovereign and legitimate power). A pronouncement is not sufficient in these matters; various conditions must be met, among them recognition from other like entities. Otherwise, how could the municipal laws in another, *foreign*, country be treated as actual laws rather than an expression of fortuitous decisions within a given constellation of power distribution? Though they are not laws for me, they are laws for someone else, and per assumption this is so in the very same sense that the laws of my country are laws for me. Another condition is that the rules that may become laws must themselves satisfy a series of conditions in order to qualify. The final source of their validity, however, is political will, which constitutes a legal person from a collective. A tacit presupposition that not everything could be an accepted and tolerated rule functions as a natural law that boundaries must exist for the process of conceiving, articulating, and formulating rules, though it is never stated where these boundaries exactly lay.[5]

However, be that as it may, sovereignty necessarily incorporates the attitude of acceptance that others may be different. This is in fact a form of tolerance that allows others the option to be different whether we find this pleasing or not (more on this later). Sovereignty refers to the authority and capacity to enforce laws on a territory, which crucially includes protecting the established order as lawful. However, what is important for us in regarding the meaning of the term "sovereignty" is that it also stands for a specific attitude—it is precisely the previously mentioned attitude of tolerance that warrants others the freedom to be different, to be their own masters. Intervention represents exactly the opposite: in its meaning it includes the presumption of authorization to cancel out precisely the entitlement embodied in one's sovereignty—or in case of human rights ideology to ignore sovereignty entirely.[6]

It is hard to imagine, however, that international peace is possible without mutual recognition of states as such. If the achievement of peace has moral value, then this implies that one must accept the condition that conflict resolution must not take an arbitrary form. Use of force would be an example of such an arbitrary form of conflict resolution, as it would be subject to the fortunes of a military action, since victory is never guaranteed.[7]

The increasing interdependence among states in the world is often cited as a justification for restricting sovereignty.[8] But interdependence as such is not incompatible with sovereignty: sovereignty in fact is grounded in recognition by others. Viewed from the perspective of international affairs, sovereignty represents a rule placing limits on foreign interference. Its role on the domestic level is, however, much more important: sovereignty expresses the presupposition that there really exists a source of authorization for the state to enforce the laws. Sovereignty is what secures the validity of the laws enforced by the state. It makes redundant demands that laws must be continually revalidated. The pluralism of states is what precludes the adoption of a specific value system, decided on in advance, as a necessary condition of legitimacy for every political order or state. A value with the special status in this context is the presupposition that valid current laws are *our* laws and not some foreign ones.[9] A demand for such an overriding value as a condition of legitimacy is in effect a demand to make the world, the whole world, uniform. According to such a view only regimes of a specific type — those representing the victorious (whether through elections or revolution) "democratic forces" — can have legitimacy.

But what regimes would these be? Are they those that have succeeded in being labeled "democratic" at the international level — even though this implies nothing about whether or not they are necessarily at all different from those that are not so labeled or indeed essentially like those that are uncontrovertibly such (i.e., democratic)? Such a requirement would not be novel. However, it does not greatly affect the basic problem: how can and should the power enforcing the laws be constituted? It appears that an important condition for that constitution is that the laws are in the first place perceived as *the laws* (even if as unjust ones) by those who are to be subjected to them, which implies that they are perceived as "our laws." How else could they be connected with any concept of justice? (If those laws were to be enforced by some extraterrestrial life — be they angels themselves — this would not be experienced, nor therefore embraced, as *one's own* law. Here lies an essential difference between law and religion: the law, whatever it may be, is specifically ours. Without this sort of loyalty there is no real possibility of the legal expression of any norm as "democratic" — foreign laws are constituted by foreigners, and we had no role in their constitution.)[10]

If it were any different, the following question would arise: who is to make decisions regarding which regimes are legitimate, and who is to be recognized as having the right to impose laws that would be recognized not only as "ours," internally speaking, but also as "alien," speaking from without? Is this to be decided domestically or from outside? If the latter, who would be in a position to make such a decision? Those who stand ready to use any means possible, including violence against people in other countries in order to decide on their behalf not only what their definition of "good" should be, but also what their "true interests" are? This approach implies global governance that requires a working world authority along with proper tools for implementing its goals, such as a world bureaucracy, world police, etc. No state, it seems, would have a right to be exempt from such an external treatment. Quite the contrary: all state-agents would have to be subjected to a continual validation process to ensure that they remain on the right path. Hence, a (world) police would play a significant role and would be endowed with immense authority. This would be in fact a political police with the authority to correct all who mistakenly refuse to listen to the official reasons why they must undertake certain actions deemed good. To be successful, this police must be equipped with the mechanisms, resources, and force of a true army. It would have to be powerful enough to enforce the peace according to the definition of "good" which concurs with these reasons. In its structure and constitution, it would look like an army while it would really be a police force, a "world police."

We must not allow this to confuse us, however. A "world police" globally authorized to enforce "political orthodoxy" would necessarily obliterate any difference between an army and the police. Its obligation to continuously search for "improprieties" would make this armed force intensively present in the social life of people. A militarized world would emerge along with a total negation of its civil character. Democracy, understood as power over oneself, however, is surely better depicted by virtue of this civil character than by becoming transfigured into a militarized-police supervision of how people think and act. This civil character, however, is fundamentally characterized by trust in others' thinking processes and actions. In the absence of clear evidence to the contrary, it is to be presumed that others' ways of thinking and acting are not wrong. This presumption of innocence, rather than of possible guilt, is what constitutes the civil character of a democratic state, which would be obliterated if a world state were to exist.

Threats, blackmail, and humiliation do not provide a proper context for respecting this presumption of innocence, not only at the domestic but also at the international level. What would remain of tolerance in the case of the development of a world police monopoly of this sort is not hard to imagine. It would not be a matter of just a monopoly — the main purpose of such a political police would be to scrutinize, continuously and in detail, everyone's orthodoxy and political correctness. Within such an environment tolerance would surely become something insupportable (as has often been the case throughout history).

Furthermore, resorting to force always leads to the incertitude of the outcome. How could one be sure that the use of force would produce exactly the desired result as a lasting situation? As a result of internal limits, force can only produce external compliance. The external compliance, however, does not come with any sincere conviction in the validity of the set goals, nor in the reasons for those goals, thus making the legitimacy of such practices questionable. If the condition of sincerity is introduced as a feature that gives final meaning to the attitude of accepting some value, things only get worse, for a resort to force is no means of fostering (or generating) sincerity. In this regard, force is powerless. Resort to force as a pattern of behavior leads to greater latitude in its use. The decision to use force often means forsaking other means of influence that may be superior though perhaps slower. The abandonment of these other forms of mutual associations—the reduction of everything to force—produces a mentality of obedience and submissiveness as well as a system of expectations within which the fear of punishment has a constitutive role. This would become the dominant feeling in place of a more comfortable attitude that punishment may naturally follow if one does wrong, but that it is equally natural to expect that one would not do wrong.

If validity of laws depended on consent from or approval by a heterogeneous source (someone presumed more powerful), then no true state authority could emerge. If states had no other venue for constituting their legitimate (domestic) authority except through acquiescence from some world superpower, then there would no longer be any valid or reliable authorities, for it can be assumed that such "acquiescence" would be forthcoming only if there existed an active interest to do so on the part of the super-power. This further implies that all characterizations of such authorities, except the momentary aptitude *vis-à-vis* the super-power, are entirely irrelevant. The very same items clearly approved of (in a particular time or place) could as easily become disapproved of or even actively condemned depending on (the latest) decisions of those who have the power to present their own interests as sentiments expressing the only relevant criterion of justice. Such essentially private justice could hardly function as a suitable or valuable foundation for constructing international legislation.

It is opportune at this point to raise the question of punishment's role as a component of intervention. The literature on humanitarian intervention entirely ignores this consideration and perceives humanitarian intervention as essentially only a rescue operation. This is to be expected and is a sure sign that humanitarian interventions should be allowed to occur only under the tightest restrictions. However, the logic embodied in the justification of humanitarian interventions we have experienced so far indicates that insisting on this constraint would amount to abandoning the mission humanitarian intervention was set out to accomplish, and hence it would be unjustified and irrational. This same logic yields the postulate of a justified punishment when human rights had been violated or democratic institutions (despite serious encouragement) were not introduced. So, the logic goes, if humanitarian intervention is justified, then a corresponding punishment for causing conditions that made the intervention necessary must also be justified.

But what must international law (and the world order) be like to make this possible? A state could only be punished if the following two conditions apply: (1) it actively fails to recognize the independence of other states, expressing this by engaging in an aggression, and (2) it is then successfully defeated.[11] Both of these conditions would be necessary (as was the case of for example, Germany at the Nuremberg trials). Punishment would then have to incorporate, among other things, the modification of that state's constitution, by explicitly introducing in the defeated aggressor's new constitution a clause recognizing the universal principle of non-aggression. Only in this fashion could a principle be shaped according to which force, even though a necessary component of law enforcement, could not as such become a rule itself.

There is a serious problem here, however. If there were no supreme coercive force—currently nonexistent in the international legal order—then, if we want to be consistent when humanitarian intervention is at stake, the following question arises. Is it permissible that a state meeting the conditions for punishment become the subject of attack by any country willing and able to engage in "corrective" activities aimed at "ameliorating" the state of affairs in that country? How could this amelioration be achieved? Can this action really be only corrective in nature? Would it not be, on the contrary, just a case wherein one country is rendering punishment on another? But how could such punishment escape the charge of amounting to private justice?

Whatever else could be said about a world state and the authorization of the universal enforcement of human rights, the consequence would be a general militarization of the world. Politics itself would become militarized: on this prescription force becomes an acceptable, highly regarded, and desirable (should we also say inexpensive?) means for accomplishing the final goal. The general militarization of global affairs would lead to the practice of an intervention becoming, rather than exceptional, quite an ordinary matter, a simple pedagogical tool, as it were, in the inventory of the New World Order. In the world as we know it, this would indicate that the practices of sending American troops around the globe would become a much more common occurrence, unsurprising to anyone.[12]

Though common, the practice thus constituted would amount to an entirely separate and irreducible factor, and, while of crucial importance at the declarative level, it would not have a constitutive role. Hence, a theoretically interesting question arises: could this crucially important factor, necessary to make the entire scheme functional, not achieve the status of a constitutive rule (though *de facto* it would already function as such a rule)? What, in other words, is the source of this need — at least on the declarative level — to negate its constitutive nature? Is it, perhaps, the fact that what in this case functions *de facto* as law cannot function also *de jure*? Or, to put it another way, if it cannot be law also in the *de jure* sense — which is the sense in which a law must be able to exist — is the practice in the final analysis unjustified? Perhaps it is the case that the law could also be expressed in the *de jure* sense, but that this is *not yet the case*, which amounts to a normative claim that it *ought to be so expressed*. But could it be? Since this law would in effect be a global law,[13] would this imply that all states would then have a duty of self-annulment in order to comply with this law? Or would this duty be reserved only for those states that had yet to live up to its demands? Which states would these be — the ones that are too weak to mount a successful defense? Or those that are not viable but unstable to a point that they trigger a reaction — for, on earth, there could only exist those states which are capable of enforcing their (own) laws?[14]

On the other hand, when considering who is a suitable party to intervene, there is not much force in the view that neighbors are unsuited to be mediators because of historically accumulated biases.[15] Quite to the contrary, neighbors predictably are better suited to understand the problems at issue than those from half a world away who rely on schemes of justice patterned after their own ideas about what the world should look like. The latter cannot hope to grasp the subtle points of the conflict, those that are frequently crucial components, for conflicts most often arise as a result of small things. Unable to grasp the subtle points of a dispute, the interventionists from far away simply apply their own thinking without penetrating into the essence of the problem. Their patterns can only be applied mechanically, and they fail to incorporate the knowledge relevant to the conflict's resolution. But the patterns are extremely suitable for ideological use, and they can quite effectively mask all kinds of interests that may emerge. (To a great extent the realization and even conceptualization of those interests depends on their remaining hidden.)

Weak States, Law Enforcement, and Defense

In light of our analysis so far, the following two scenarios might provide solid grounds for military intervention. First, a state may be enforcing laws that are intolerable (this was the justification given *ex post facto* for the intervention of Tanzania in Uganda). Second, a state might be nearly or entirely powerless to enforce its own laws effectively across its entire territory, leaving pockets where laws systematically go unenforced or competing laws may exist within its borders, a potentially objectionable situation from the international-legal point of view. The latter might have been, at least in part, applicable to the case of the Kosovo intervention that came after a decade of lawlessness. This was manifest in the parallel functioning of two systems of power and, for all intents and purposes, two parallel states. What emerges as a problem in such cases is the proper understanding of the term "humanitarian" in those contexts. If we used the term "humanitarian intervention" to refer to the cases of perhaps justified instances of intervention of the second kind we would depart from the prototypical usage of the term associated with gross violations of human rights, as exemplified, for instance, by Walzer.[16]

This brings us full circle, however, to the idea that states come into existence only where there is enough will and power to enact some law. If this will and power are present, then this constitutes an established fact not unlike a victorious end to a war. The alternative to this is to view every expression of any autonomous legislative will as automatically constituting a criminal act from the point of a — still nonexistent — world state "constitution," i.e., as a harm to the authority of that center of power which is the strongest in the whole world. The strongest in what sense, we might ask: that it is recognized as such, seen as such, or that it is merely threatening to punish every disobedience? But even if there were such recognition, what could be objectionable about a group of people who decide to put together their own separate state somewhere at the edge of the world? Could they be expressing disrespect toward the source of universal laws? But who could have the pretension to be such a "source"? It appears that such a pretension implies the assumption of infallibility, which is epistemologically unacceptable.[17] If, however, we searched for the sources of the (potential) global law in the same places that currently ground all existing laws — some legislative will — the following question would still remain to be answered. Is the will of the stronger in itself, as such, a source of a legitimization for the set goals, or, on the contrary, is such legitimization itself in need of justification? Or, to rephrase it slightly: where are, if any, the limits to the will of the stronger in this legitimization process? Does legitimization need some *independent reasons* to be valid? Or is the will of the stronger already such a "prevailing reason"?[18]

This deliberation occurs against the background of an assumption that there is no danger of another world war. With this in the background, decisions to undertake smaller "actions" are immensely facilitated. Even the prevailing language indicates a peculiar shift away from "war" to "smaller actions" allegedly distinct from war. The very term "war" is all but eliminated from official discourse (certainly in the vocabulary concerning humanitarian intervention) and replaced by terms that indicate in advance which side is allegedly in the right. Terms like "aggression," "action," and "campaign" are increasingly ubiquitous. The former is presumably outlawed by regulations of international law, particularly by the Convention of the United Nations.

The latter terms should indicate that warfare or military action is not occurring but, rather, a police action (regardless of the fact that an army is far more involved than the police). Even various (social) experiments are contemplated and referred to by terms like "peace-keeping," "peace-enforcing" (which should further strengthen the impression that supposedly a police "action" is at work), and even "peace-making" — which, as far as the meaning of the phrase could go, designates precisely war.

The sole remaining thing with a remote war-like character that must be eliminated is aggression, not as a word but as an offensive, and for that matter criminal, act. This is precisely why the side that finds itself under attack is labeled as the aggressor. However, the goal in this is not victory, but the ability to dictate specific sorts of behavior to those who are desired to be influenced. Since it is not war that is at stake, victory is unimportant. This provides enormous maneuvering room for retreat; it is possible at any moment (as can be seen from the case of Somalia and perhaps even of Vietnam if we look at it more carefully from the angle of subsequent developments and envisage retreat as a goal of the presumably "defeated" side). Victory, in fact, could not even exist—for defeat is impossible! It could not even be envisaged as a possible option. And by excluding victory and defeat—as "war-like" characteristics of the conflict—the notion of an "enemy" is also eliminated (even though it is still used, but only from inertia, in the jargon of the mass media), which then clears the path toward total universal benevolence. Since the goal is not victory but achievement of the best effect, there can be no limits to possible progress either. In fact, no limits exist to the use of any means that could lead to the goal. The goal justifies any means and actually demands the use of the most efficient ones. It is clear the most efficacious means would be the use of overwhelming force. Thus, force becomes indistinguishable from politics. There is no shying away from any means. (Any means? Does that include manipulation, lies, and propaganda, if they happen to be best means? There is nothing contradictory in these being, in fact, the best means.) Readiness to use force becomes something positive, a sign of attentiveness to making progress. In any case, this should also be covered by the principle of rationality, for this is simply a matter of someone who is unwavering in selecting a goal choosing the best means for reaching it. All of this gets further psychological support in the context of the above-mentioned fact that no serious military attack from any direction seems possible and is certainly not expected.

Supremacy

These considerations may perhaps also be understood in terms of a disposition to secure the *maximum* security that one can achieve *in advance*. Imperial politics always includes among its goals *security*, which for the sake of accomplishing high aspirations on a wide—even global—scale requires continuous monitoring, alertness, and (combat) readiness. This implies *domination*. One way to achieve dominance is certainly through (military) superiority, as a strategic position incorporates the stance that in no situation can there be a question of who is stronger. In this way the set of chosen foundational values is very strongly protected by supplying a notion of "justice" that affords it a principled and mighty defense. Legitimacy is thus secured both internally (via the notion of consent) and externally (via the notion of injustice that serves to annul any factually legitimating process existing as a result of, perhaps only servile, prior acceptance of a *different* value system than the one protected by the presupposition of this supremacy). Injustice is not simply a matter of encroaching those constraints that the more powerful can *illegally* mete out to the weaker (in the sense that this would violate some "strong," i.e., legitimate, interests of the latter), but there also exists the presupposition about the strongest one, the one who "most intensely cares about everything"—who will ensure that all legitimate interests are respected and illegitimate ones are punished. This is a description of the most extreme situation, of course, but it is the direction in which the logic of this "ensuring" leads. Thus, the *monopoly* on power becomes (in a fashion similar to how it secures the internal legitimization of law) in some sense a logical consequence of "imperialism," not only that power obtains the supreme evaluative role (including the right to be offended by others' acts that deviate from what "we" regard as "just"), but also that a transition to factually *secure* this position is effected. This presupposes *supremacy*, not only with respect to (earthly) evaluative processes, but also with respect to (pure) force. Liberalism and democracy, hence, no longer have their basis in autonomy. In their places comes *one* among many possible *interpretations* of content that could be subsumed under those concepts. This interpretation then advances in the form of a *political force* with its altogether specific political program its foundation. This political program becomes the final basis of all legitimization and, given its distinct nature, every deviation is defined as "injustice." This circumstance manufactures conflict that can be "controlled" only through securing the supremacy over all other sides in this universal conflict. Supremacy appears necessary in order to realize the "unity of the idea of justice." It must be adequate to produce dominance, and, if insufficient to prevent conflicts, must be able to ensure they cannot escape control, or (worse) that their outcomes become uncertain, leaving the possibility open for "the other side to prevail."

Initially this is embodied in the strategic purpose of any military—that it be ready to successfully repel any attack. This purpose would be secured with certainty if one had an army that were superior to every other army. However, whenever war is possible, this kind of success cannot be guaranteed, so war would have to be abolished altogether. Overwhelming force would be required, with a single and absolute military superiority. It appears quite logical that choosing to intervene in such circumstances would become a great deal easier for two reasons. First, the reduced (and relativized) cost of intervention would make this decision easier. Second, because the whole decision-making process would be affected by this (low cost of intervention) an additional "reason" would be produced that would both facilitate the decision and generate a sense of "mission," a call "to do something" that is not only possible but also easy. All this is embedded in the logic of globalization: that the entire world become subsumed under a single measure, with rules that make the world into a network of influences that will "solidify and secure world peace." The presumption of general value commensurability that emerges from this unification process leads to the conclusion that everything that is simultaneously good, easy to achieve, and generates no conflict with other values if realized, therefore, ought to be realized. Absence of principled conflicts between values implies a maximalist pretension that the totality of the possible "good" really be actualized, *hic et nunc*. In this picture ruling the world becomes almost a "science," while politicians resemble benevolent experts who make sacrifices for the sake of those they rule, and again in two senses: because they decide for them (for they know what is good), and because they then execute those decisions, often over unreasonable reluctance from those on whose behalf they make sacrifices. The key difference remains, however, between the (globally unified) "avant-guard" and the complex (heterogeneous) remainder of the world (comprised of those who are to be "helped" and "defended").

There are two important points here. First, those who break rules are perceived as presenting danger that merits no toleration, and respect for the rules governing the distribution of influence is *sine qua non* for membership in the "world community." This membership, of course, is primarily important because it saves one from being a possible target of attack. Second, when there is total superiority over all others, the term "defense" loses all meaning. This is a very peculiar situation, for if there were no defense everything it presupposes should also become absolutely redundant: the ends of defense such as the state and its borders as well as the means of defense, such as standing armies and weapons. This is the corollary of the prescription implicit in the process of globalization or one of its goals. If defense were no longer needed, everything would be transposed on the positive axis of human activity; everything would be done for the sake of positive values of well being, prosperity, and happiness. There would be nothing to be "defended."

The question, however, is whether this brings more security or less (even though security is not included among the fundamental values of globalization, having been on a lower level than prosperity, democracy, etc.). We may consider whether or not globalization could be accomplished without a decisive role for the US military. Taking seriously the logic of globalization and what was just stated above, two more questions might be raised. First, should the US intervene even in, for example, China? The question that is posed by Walzer[19] in this context must be generalized to this level of "generality." Furthermore, if the answer is positive, the logic above dictates the second question. What is a greater danger for peace: coercive enforcement of democracy (with the aim of enhancing universal prosperity along the way)[20] or acceptance and living with the fact that others are different? The latter amounts to tolerating the unpleasant situation that others choose to shape their lives collectively, not only individually, in ways different from ours. Even assuming that the concept of justice is the same all around the globe—that there is no *principled* differentiation among collectives with respect to their basic goals (and that all disputes concern only the means for those ends) and that these collectives are not "moral strangers"[21]—it does not follow in the political sense that the world ought to be united. These collectives, as actual ongoing forms of life, certainly will experience direct conflict over the realization of the same goals (each wanting to take the fruits of this realization for themselves).[22] Moreover, the concrete articulations of these per assumption identical goals will obtain different forms with the passage of time, created of varying traditions.

In the end, there remains the question: is universal peace guaranteed once all countries become democracies? Or is more required, such as that all countries become affluent? Or is it something more than that? Perhaps even this would be insufficient, and what would be required is for the entire world to become just one state. But, as an author noted, crusades mean a lot of labor for soldiers,[23] and "full spectrum dominance" is certainly a sufficiently removed goal that much work remains to be done along the way to achieving it.

Promotion of Human Rights as a Reason for Internationalizing Internal Conflicts

Ascertaining violations of human rights is not a simple matter of empirical inquiry. In order for these violations to be identified an interpretation is necessary, and it might often be the case that the applied interpretation depends on factors, invisible at first sight, which render it defective or inadequate. Should such an interpretation lead to radical inferences the resulting mistakes may be enormous. Often a selection is made among many pertinent factors ruling some of them more or less definitionally important for a given case, which could lead to a very biased, skewed, partial, or incorrect picture of the real state of affairs. Since the inferences in question deal with very important matters, making them could lead to extremely serious, long-term, negative consequences. Though tolerance may be among the proclaimed ideals, nurturing respect for the different ways life is organized remains a tedious, burdensome objective. Foreign and alien (e.g., "non-democratic") ways of life can be susceptible to an "excess of interpretation," as well as to a "deficiency" of interpretation, but always with significant, often far-reaching consequences.

To take an example, consider an attempt to fulfill a most sincere and powerful desire for self-determination. It is almost inevitable that actions associated with this sort of attempt will lead to conflicts that may be perceived from afar as violations of human rights in the sense that there are those whose perhaps genuine and strong desires may get stifled and suppressed. It may be that actions motivated by a drive for self-determination get punished, not necessarily with disproportionate severity, but perhaps seemingly so. Or it may appear that they are even suppressed by means that are neither enjoyable nor entirely morally defensible. However, it is quite possible that the same matter, when scrutinized in its immediate environment, or within one's own state, could give rise to an entirely opposite perception that what is occurring is a simple matter of enforcing the laws of the land in the most usual manner. The perception may not be any different than the perception of the enforcement of tax laws, for example, that may include forced payments, which in many circumstances is very unpleasant for all involved and often is even morally suspect. Is this a projection of one's own way of life onto others? That is not clear, but it need not be. But neither need this be the application of a double standard—one evaluation for "us," another for "them." Instead, this may simply be a result of differing perceptions that fail to incorporate, purposefully or not, precisely those elements of similarity and regard only those that lead to the conclusion that something unpleasant and wrong is going on. If it so happens that the bearer of this perception is the one who is in the position to intervene, or one who feels called upon to do so—and who in the contemporary circumstance of the univocal media is in fact delegated to "do something"—then this will significantly affect the process of decision-making so that the application of a double standard will become, as it were, a corollary of the blunder contained in the initial perception itself. When this is compounded with the perhaps natural propagandist tendency toward exaggeration, and, perhaps also natural, but certainly immoral, desire for choosing a side in someone else's fight, then a peculiar spiral of evil may emerge resulting in the (unsanctioned) enjoyment in the suffering of strangers. All the while this enjoyment is expressed in the lynch-mob-like scream that "something must be done," that the "something" must be drastic in nature (as compared to what is presented as a problem), and that those who "must" do that something are "we ourselves." The whole thing, however, may be that we are dealing with actions that incorporate conflicts and result in various rights violations perhaps involving all agents in the conflict.[24] That is, these may include violations of the rights of both those who break the law and those who try to enforce it, perhaps using violence, encountering all the while a disproportionate and unnatural resistance to the performance of their *work duties*.

All of this, when occurring elsewhere, can quite easily be experienced as a violation of someone's human rights, while similar situations at home are treated as routine responses to violations of the law. Consequently, it often appears that intervention, in situations when the targets are weak states with weak authorities,[25] is a "solution" to a problem that represents not only interference with internal affairs, but also a drastic negation of domestic legislation, i.e., the very same thing that the intervening sides in their own countries scrupulously respect. Hence, the very same items that are at home regarded as lawful handling of rebellion and/or criminal activity are seen in other countries as violations of human rights.

In this context, two relevant possibilities ought to be mentioned. First, it might be an element of the strategy of the rebelling side to send a message to the world that violations of human rights are occurring, and, regardless of the fact that this may really be the case, the *goal* of this strategy—perfectly rational from the stance of the rebels or potential rebels—may be something else. Instead of focusing on the source of the problem (which in some cases also may lead to conflict, but more often leads to an emerging need to address the problem and find a solution to the conflict), the strategic goal may be to generate wide sympathy and support for "the cause." Second, a latent conflict may become inflamed (and the need arises to send out to the world compelling messages about human rights violations for the sake of this same goal of generating sympathy and support) because an opportunity for it is quickly snapped parasitizing on some other (usually larger) conflict. An example of this is that of the Iraqi Kurds, who were successful in conjoining their tendency toward self-determination and self-rule to the larger political situation of the Gulf "War." What is particularly interesting here is how much attention has been given to the human rights violations of the Iraqi Kurds in the writings of authors who deal with human rights, which is dramatically disproportional to the lack of attention to, arguably, the considerably more serious human rights situation the Kurds have faced in Turkey, for example.[26]

Conclusion

The pro-interventionist stance, justified in terms of the promotion of human rights, in light of our analysis, therefore, has the following two defects: (1) it functions as a continuous generator of increasingly frequent conflicts; and (2) it creates the requirement that there be some supreme authority that would have at its disposal adequate capabilities to apply coercive force wherever needed. Adequate capabilities in this context, of course, imply having a massive military might, since in its absence the authority to use coercive force could not amount to much. The need for a supreme coercive force is based not only on the natural mistrust that always exists among people requiring extra security measures, but even more on the heterogeneity of the world bitterly resisting any unification in the department of ideals. Furthermore, a single authority is also required in order to provide for the possibility that interventions be interpreted as defensive actions. It is not possible to treat the combating of human rights violations as a sort of defense unless there exists a unique point of reference fully authorized to interpret situations without allowance for appeals. Otherwise who should instigate and complete the intervention becomes questionable. As things stand in the current international legal order, states are those entities responsible for making final decisions about whether to intervene or not. Given that sovereignty represents a regulative rule that is required for law to be constituted within a territory (though sovereignty itself is never "absolute"), and given that the existence of states in the world has its moral and political justification, it is unlikely that in the future humans will do away with states.

If, however, all municipal laws require, in order to be valid, an imprimatur of and authorization from an "international authority" (not necessarily in the sense that they are legislated by this authority, but in the sense that the latter authority could—temporarily or permanently—revoke or cancel laws implemented by any given domestic authority), then, assuming the nonexistence of the world state, no law could be perceived as reliably binding. The purpose of law, however, is precisely to offer protection—including, among other things, by making it clear what is legal and what is not. The purpose of this is to offer guarantees for exactly those freedoms that a given society has selected for such protection. If validity of law depended on an *ad hoc* approval from someone presumed more powerful—if states inherently had no other source for constituting the legitimacy of internal rulers except through approval from a world super-power—then there would no longer be any solid or reliable state-power.[27]

Thus we return to the basic question: does tolerance mean leaving others alone to decide how they will regulate their lives as collectives as well as individuals, or does tolerance mean insisting on providing all options to all people on every corner of the globe? In other words, everything turns on the definition of the term "pluralism." What does it mean? Does it mean preserving a variety of social orders (societies that differ one from another) or constructing a united world that will contain just one "society" that "overcomes" social differences, in order to tolerate individual differences? It appears that it is the latter that the doctrine of human rights professes and demands.[28]

Notes

1. Cf. M. Walzer, "The Politics of Rescue," *Social Research* 62.1 (Spring 1995); B. Williams, "Is International Rescue a Moral Issue," *Social Research* 62.1 (Spring 1995).

2. For this discrepancy, see J. Shand Watson, *Theory and Reality in the International Protection of Human Rights* (Ardsley, NY: Transnational Publishers, 1999), especially chapter IX.

3. This permission is, ex hypothesi, not primary but parasitical on the antecedent principled prohibition of that sort of action.

4. Cf. I. Kant, *Metaphysik der Sitten*, pars, 46, 47; *Metaphysics of Morals*, trans. Mary Gregor (Cambridge: Cambridge University Press, 1991) 91, 92: "The legislative authority can belong only to the united will of the people"; "... superior [authority] over all ... from the viewpoint of laws of freedom can be none other than the united people itself."

5. That the boundary must exist is perfectly clear, however, and can be further clarified by the fact that various rules could be envisaged which cannot be constituted—or tolerated—as laws. The notion that this boundary must exist is the source that generates universalism of the pretension in those norms contained in the doctrine of human rights according to which those rights are everywhere and always identical. However, that is not so; simply because there exists a boundary applicable to the possibility that certain rules could be constituted into laws, it does not follow that those rules are everywhere true. What does follow is that there are rules such that their eventual pretension to count as laws or to be declared as laws would be null and void. Thus a minimal universality is preserved—in the negative form, as a principle that determines this boundary beyond which we have rules that cannot be recognized and/or tolerated. But also preserved are diversity, variability, and differences that result from tolerance and from a rejection of the pretension that only "our laws" are really laws. Determining this boundary is of course a very difficult task, both theoretically and practically—this should not surprise us, as it presupposes defining a boundary beyond which tolerance is no longer justified. Theoretically speaking, there is a sense in which this demarcation can and cannot be made: a principle could be articulated according to which this determination is made, but a concrete decision is a matter of moral practice and presupposes a certain responsibility, which could hardly exist if the point of the boundary were to be determined "deductively" by logical necessity from some description of the given state of affairs. This seems to be a general characteristic of moral evaluation, and implies that making a decision in the moral context always incorporates the taking of some moral risk. But it also opens, rather than closes, the space for acting in ways that may turn out right or wrong, so that it could never be known in advance with absolute certainty which they are.

6. The ignoring of sovereignty may not be necessary, in fact. It stems from the assumption that the final and precise list of "human rights," along with their definite description, can be given, in order to accomplish the outcome that this theory—once it starts functioning as an ideology—generates: the motivation that these rights, as basic, be "secured for all." What creates a problem here is not the term "rights," nor in a certain minimal sense the term "secure" (though the latter is an enormous problem because there is a requirement to articulate a viable conception of justice that could be cosmopolitan), but is rather the term "all." Does this term

stand for "all" as equals (which is implied by the finality of the list and by the definiteness of the description of "human rights") or does it refer to "all" who are here, who really exist, and who are the way they are: free and fallible—which mutually imply each other.

7. It is possible, however, that a strategy might be formulated that would to a large extent reduce the importance of this factor of arbitrariness. In a way this is the case with the current US military doctrine of "overwhelming force" that tends to completely exclude this factor. What stands in the way is the third factor from the triad that determines the human position in the world: temporality (the triad consists of freedom, finality, and temporality). Conditions might arise for the application of such a strategy. But, given that these factors represent only the basis for constructing any values at all, while those values gain their motivational force—in the form of interests—through much more complex sets of influencing factors, there could not be an advanced "securing the security" of human rights to "all," even according to this rough description. The intervention in Somalia quite clearly shows this. Though it was conceived by all accounts as humanitarian in nature, the motivation, however, could not endure to realization—for the part that deals with "securing" (in this case some humanitarian goals) is always just one among many mutually competing interests. The ideology of human rights is forced to presuppose the impossible: that in any set of interests, securing basic human rights is ultimately the strongest interest always and in all places.

8. But also those who favor "abolishing" sovereignty don't ever say where it would "go." That is, they fail to offer reasons describing how the elimination of sovereignty from a nation and its transplantation elsewhere is anything other than usurpation. Nor do they tell us what sorts of features the elite absorbing it would have to have so that this action wouldn't be usurpation—how this would be something different than a simple transposition of sovereignty to a more powerful side.

9. Foreign laws may not only be perceived as better than the ones in the land of the perceiver, but according to all parameters really be better. That will in no way change things. The conquerors of the world as occupiers have always had to face this matter anew. When, for example, Napoleon's France (marching in the name of all-inclusive human progress) conquered Spain, five years of resistance ensued (until the French were driven out of Spain in 1813), which to many may have appeared irrational and backward; even in Spain itself a movement, "Afrancesados," existed whose members saw themselves as a "progressive elite" saluting and supporting the perspective of modernization that the French were bringing along, maintaining that this was better for Spain than the backward state of affairs existing then. Still, the mass of the Spaniards "preferred, in effect, to be backward and Spanish rather than progressive and Frenchifying." See Geoffrey Best, *Humanity in Warfare* (London: Weidenfeld and Nicolson, 1980) 114-15.

10. Hence, even the enforcement of the "divine justice" on earth is doomed to be illegal in the most relevant sense of the word and this ought to be the principal achievement of the secular emancipation in the progress of mankind. For example, The Holy Inquisition may have appeared just and in its form "lawful," or "legal" but that form is false; this is why its judgments are illegal even when they are just.

11. Cf. J. Babic, "War Crimes: Moral, Legal, or Simply Political?," *War Crimes and Collective Wrongdoing: A Reader*, ed. A. Jokic (Oxford: Blackwell, 2001).

12. Speaking of means, Walzer avers: "In many cases nothing at all will be done unless we (US) are prepared to play one or the other of these parts—either the political lead or a combination of financial backer and supporting player. Old and well-earned suspicions of American power must give way now to a wary recognition of its necessity." (Walzer at this point adds a very curious constraint, that this optimism wouldn't be so warranted if "there

were a Republican president"!) See Walzer 64-65. Similarly Richard Haas apologetically states: "On balance, ... the question of US military intervention becomes more rather than less commonplace and more rather than less complicated"; R.N. Haas, *Intervention: The Use of American Military Force in the Post-Cold War World*, Washington, D.C: Brookings Institution Press, 1999) 2. A.J. Bachevich, critically observes: "...the American military establishment will assert itself proactively to 'shape' the international environment"; Andrew A. Bachevich, "Policing Utopia. The Military Imperatives of Globalization," *The National Interest* (Summer 1999): 8.

13. The need for a supreme power of enforcement, so characteristic of the "constitutive" aspect of law (hence the dialectic between the "regulative" and "constitutive" legal norms can never achieve the level of full universality, as in morality) is not satisfied at the international level. This need comes from the impossibility of avoiding distrust, and this lack of trust makes the legal norms (laws) into something very different from planning (though the way I have defined them here, given that legal norms express some political decision, i.e., decisions of some legislative will, they could appear to be just that: projections, decisions about the ways to act, which actions will be obligatory, which forbidden, and which only permissible).

14. Cf. e.g., Richard Falk: "The main challenges are associated with the dynamics of 'the weak state' unable to sustain order within its territorial boundaries rather than with the traditional focus of international relations on the expansionist machinations of 'the strong state'"; R. Falk, "'Humanitarian Wars': Realist Geopolitics, and Genocidal Practices: 'Saving the Kosovars,'" n.p. 1. Cf. also T. Langford, "Things Fall Apart: State Failure and the Politics of Intervention," *International Studies Review* 1 (1999).

15. See, e.g., Walzer 55.

16. Walzer.

17. See note 11, above.

18. Cf. B. Williams, "In the Beginning Was the Deed," *Deliberative Democracy and Human Rights*, ed. H.H. Koh and R.C. Slye (New Haven, CT, and London: Yale University Press, 1999).

19. See note 13, above.

20. Michael Smith: "we could solve many problems throughout the world just by the use of good will and the dispatching of peace keepers wherever they might be necessary ... to intervene on behalf of democratic legitimacy—to create democratically legitimate states everywhere"; Michael Smith, "Humanitarian Intervention: An Overview of the Ethical Issues," *Ethics and International Affairs* 12 (1998): 66.

21. Cf. A. Buchanan, Chapter 7, this volume, p. 140-01.

22. For the idea that the agreement with respect to goals, i.e., interests, does not lead to harmony, but to conflict, see I. Kant, *Critique of Practical Reason*, trans. H.W. Cassirer (Milwaukee, WI: Marquette University Press, 1998) 30 (Ak. 28): "The desire for happiness is universal, and so is the *maxim* by virtue of which that desire is made by each man a determining ground of his will. Still ... the effect of one's wishing to bestow upon that maxim the universality of a law would be very opposite of harmony... The harmony this results in resembles that encountered in a certain satirical poem which describes the harmony subsisting between two marriage partners bent on each other's ruin in the following words, '*Oh, what wondrous harmony, whene'er he wants a thing, so does she...*' Or else, one is reminded of the story we are told about the arrogant claim made by King Francis I against the Emperor Charles V, when he is said, 'What my brother Charles wants [viz. Milan] I want too.'"

23. Cf. Bachevich 12.

24. Thus, through forceful secessions and wars that emerged on that basis in former Yugoslavia, Serbia found itself without its seaports, just as its citizens are no longer able to vacation at usual seaside resorts without the burdensome and humiliating process of getting visas. With the destruction of structures and of the relations developed and nurtured for almost a century, these are just two minor harms of many that occurred. Is harming others a violation of their rights? It need not be the case, but it might. The point is that whether or not harms done will also be rights violations—no matter how minor or insignificant they may appear—cannot be predetermined.

25. See note 15, above.

26. A drastic example of this can be seen in the previously mentioned article by Michael Smith, where enormous attention is given to the plight of Iraqi Kurds who are denied their right of self-determination, while Turkish Kurds *are not even mentioned* as if they do not exist at all! In examples like this one it is almost impossible to avoid the question of what exactly is the ultimate goal of the authors who exhibit this level of partisanship.

27. It can be assumed that such permission will be forthcoming only if an adequate interest for it exists. This further implies that all other characteristics of this regime, besides its suitability expressed through its obedience, may be irrelevant: the same thing may receive approval or disapproval (or even condemnation), on the basis of a decision made by those who can present their interests in the form of sentiments that represent the criterion of justice: such essentially private justice can hardly provide a sound basis for international law.

28. The research for this paper was supported by a grant from MacArthur Foundation's Program on Global Security and Sustainability. I am grateful to the following friends and colleagues for their suggestions and assistance: Aleksandar Jokic, Wendy Rea Doggett, Bob Gillis, and Milan Brdar.

4

Humanitarian Intervention and Moral Theory

Michael Philips

Introduction

In this paper I will describe two fundamentally different ways of thinking about morality and moral philosophy and will examine the ways in which they influence our approach to the question of humanitarian intervention. I call the first "The Metaphysical Conception of Morality" and the second "The Instrumental Conception." These "conceptions" are not themselves moral theories. They are not and they do not entail action guiding principles (i.e., principles of the kind "one ought to do A" or "it is wrong to do B"). Strictly speaking, they belong to metaethics, not ethics. In particular, they provide us with coherent pictures of the nature of morality itself, our attitudes towards morality, and the way moral standards are properly justified. I believe that these pictures shape the work of many philosophers and that they influence much ordinary thinking about morality.

The elements of these pictures are mutually supporting in the sense that they provide arguments and explanations for one another. A given philosopher might subscribe to certain elements of both pictures without contradicting herself, but she would be faced with difficult questions that do not arise on the purer conceptions. In some cases, moreover, this would create serious tensions in her work.

Serious discussions of the nature of morality itself and the role it plays in human life have been long out of fashion in English-language philosophy. Many philosophers do take positions on the various assumptions constitutive of these conceptions at various places in their work, but little explicit thought is devoted to defending at least many of the assumptions I will discuss, and little attention is devoted to situating them in some wider conception of the nature and purpose of morality. Rather, to the extent that these assumptions are considered at all by most philosophers, they are considered on an issue-by-issue basis. If I am right, this means that much thinking about moral questions is influenced by coherent background pictures of which their authors are not aware. My task is to describe these two very influential sets of background assumptions and to examine how they affect our approach to questions of international relations in general and humanitarian intervention in particular.

Before beginning, I should note that the distinction between the metaphysical conception and the instrumental conception is not meant to replace the main distinction philosophers employ to divide ethical theories, namely, the distinction between deontic theories and teleological theories. I will discuss the relation between these sets of distinctions later in this paper.

The Metaphysical Conception

In a justly famous essay "Modern Moral Philosophy," G.E.M. Anscombe argues that much moral philosophy in the modern period is an attempt to retain the most important elements of religious ethics while rejecting God.[1] That is, secular philosophers reject that old-time religion, but want to retain important features of the morality it supported. Although my understanding of how this works is somewhat different from hers, I think her insight at least partly explains the appeal of the metaphysical conception. It represents a kind of nostalgia for the moral comforts and certainty of religious morality without its apparently arbitrary and outmoded content. It is an attempt to retain as much of the structure of religious morality as one can while substituting Reason for God.

The following sketch is meant to convey the spirit of this view. It ignores many unclarities and ambiguities that lurk beneath the surface. Many of these are of interest only to professional philosophers. I discuss some of them in the notes.

According to the metaphysical conception, morality is the most important dimension of human life. Moral conceptions always trump considerations of other kinds.[2] We must do the right thing or the just thing no matter what the consequences are. We must be willing to surrender our own happiness, even our own lives for the sake of morality.

Thus Alan Gewirth writes:

Persons guide their lives in many different ways. Among the various goals, rules, habits, ideals, and institutions that figure more or less explicitly in such guidance morality has a unique status. For it purports to set for everyone's conduct requirements that take precedence over all other modes of guiding action, including even the self-interest of the person to whom it is addressed.[3]

And D.Z. Philips:

> Moral considerations are, for the man who cares for them, the most
> important of all considerations ... the demands of morality are un-
> conditional in that they cannot be put aside for considerations of
> another kind.[4]

Taken by itself, this view is rather mysterious. Why should anyone hold one
ought never to tell a relatively minor lie (e.g., on one's resume) to secure a
substantial personal gain (e.g., a good job)? One answer to this is the time-
honored moralist view that honoring moral principles makes one a better
person. In fact, it is what matters most in evaluating persons (and may even be
all that matters). A second feature of the metaphysical conception, then, is that
moral worth is our most cherished treasure. We learn from Socrates that the
only true harm we can suffer is the harm that comes of doing wrong. We learn
from Kant that the only thing that is unconditionally good—good in itself—is
the good will, the will that is in conformity to moral law. The shock and even
outrage that greeted Susan Wolf's paper "Moral Saints" suggests that this assumption is alive and well in many quarters of the philosophical community.[5]

A third feature of the metaphysical conception is that morality is a self-
standing, independent metric of moral worth. The principles of morality
describe what we must do or be to earn it or to lose it. That is the point of
morality; it has and needs no other. In fact, any further purpose introduces the
possibility of conflicts with this one. If morality also took promoting prosperity to be a goal, the standards that measure moral worth might conflict with the
standards generated by that additional goal. Furthermore, it would be difficult
to explain the supremacy of the moral: we can always ask why principles generated by goals like promoting prosperity should take precedence over considerations of other kinds (e.g., promoting humor or aesthetic appreciation).
If we subscribe to these components of the metaphysical conception, we have
a problem unless we take moral worth to be something we possess as persons
that is relatively independent of the contingencies of our historical situation.
The quest for moral worthiness, however, stands above all competitors. Our
success or failure constitutes the basis on which God would judge (if there
were a God). The principles of morality tell us how to measure our success or
failure.

Since morality is about moral worthiness, the principles of morality bind
unconditionally. That is, our level of commitment to them is not contingent
on anyone else's level of commitment to them. That is a fourth feature of the
metaphysical conception. No matter how evil and depraved the rest of the
world may be, our primary concern is to be good. It may be costly to us to

act morally in a morally depraved world; however, since moral principles are supreme, and since moral worth is our most treasured possession, this is precisely what is required of us.

Since the principles of morality tell us what it is for a human being to have moral worth, they must apply to us as human beings (or persons). At some level of abstraction, at least, they must be the same for men and women, investment bankers and native shamen, Ancient Greeks and contemporary Puerto Ricans. There may be some variations due to local conditions, traditions, and social structures, but all local variations must be justified in relation to higher level principles that apply to everyone. These higher level principles allow us to say what lower level principles are justified, given local conditions. These higher level principles are universal. That is a fifth feature of this model.

Of course, it would be pointless to claim that moral principles are measures of our worth and should be acted on even at great personal expense unless it were possible to discover what these principles are. At very least it would be strange to say, "One should make any sacrifice necessary for the sake of morality, but, by the way, no one knows what morality requires of us. Do what you think is right, maybe you'll get lucky." So it is difficult to motivate the metaphysical conception unless one also believes that sincere, reasonably intelligent people willing to do some intellectual work can determine what morality requires of us. That they can is a sixth feature of this model. This is not to say that the task is easy. The stakes are often high and we may be subject to so many distorting influences (e.g., partisan feelings and other emotional attachments). Objectivity is an achievement not easily won, but, if we can get ourselves into a cool and dispassionate state of mind, if we can divorce ourselves from all partisan concerns, and if we can reason effectively, we can discover the truths about morality.

The metaphysical conception is generally accompanied by a moral epistemology, an account of how these discoveries can be made. Although there are differences in the details, the core idea is that we can arrive at moral truths by means of philosophical reflection. The simplest versions are intuitionist.[6] They hold that just as we can consult our intuitions to determine whether one step in an argument follows from another, or to determine that $2 + 2 = 4$, so we can consult our intuitions to determine truths in ethics. Roughly, it works like this. In our calm, dispassionate hours, we assemble a set of moral judgments in which we have great confidence (for example, torturing George W. Bush against his will for the fun of it is wrong). We go on to look for the set of principles that explain these judgments (for example, it is wrong to cause pain in others against their will just for one's own enjoyment). We may also consult our intuitions about principles. This process does not always operate smoothly. It may turn out that some of our intuitions support a principle while others seem to oppose it. In these cases our job is to arrive at a set of principles that is supported to the highest degree possible by our intuitions.

Some metaphysical moralists rely on a more deductivist or analytical approach. Inspired by Kant, they take the supreme principle of morality to be that persons must be respected. And they try to generate the rest of morality by reflecting on what that principle means, that is, by reflecting on the nature of persons and/or the nature of respect.[7] In either case, the metaphysical moralist believes that through the careful and dispassionate application of the tools of moral philosophy, we can discover the principles of morality.

In some cases, we may believe that a principle is true without knowing quite what it asserts. For example, we may believe that sexism is wrong without quite being able to say what sexism is. The metaphysical moralist believes that there is a truth of this matter as well and that that truth can be discovered by the tools of philosophical analysis. An accurate analysis of sexism tells us what sexism really is.

It is clear that the metaphysical conception needs a moral epistemology. Given the fact that moral views differ so widely across time and place, anyone who argues that there is some ahistorical metric of moral worth (or some set of principles binding on rational beings as such) owes us an account of how to discover it. Although one can subscribe to the "rationalist" moral epistemology associated with the metaphysical conception without adopting the whole package, there is also a way in which that epistemology relies on features of that model, for without those features, it would be hard to understand the importance of the moral principles delivered by that epistemology. Without the idea that morality is a metric of moral worth, those standards would at best be mere dictates of reason. As such it is hard to see why they should take precedence over other dictates of reason (e.g., prudential considerations). More importantly, it is hard to see why we should respond differently to murderers than we do to people who are irrational in other ways (e.g., who discount base rates in probability assessments). If we take morality to be the measure of moral worth (and hence human worth), we do not have this problem.

In sum, the metaphysical conception holds that there are a set of moral principles, binding on rational agents as such, that are sufficient for the moral life. These principles constitute a self-standing metric that allows us to measure our own moral worth and the worth of others. Since moral worth is our most cherished possession, these principles are supremely important; that is, they take precedence over all other considerations in cases of conflict. The term "Morality" functions as a proper name for that set of principles. There is just one true morality, and it is discoverable. The job of moral philosophers is to discover it.

The Instrumental Conception

According to the instrumentalist, there is no such thing as Morality with an upper case "M." There are only moralities. The term "Morality" is not a proper name that stands for a unique set of principles, but rather a general term for a social institution or a code of personal conduct. Just as there is not one true Language, but many languages, there is not one true Morality but many moralities. These moralities are not self-standing measures of some universal quality or property called moral worth, which is something that, like mathematical ability, is the same wherever it appears. Rather, like languages, moralities have a purpose (or purposes). The point of a social morality is to promote and to protect a reasonably valued way of life (that is, a way of life that realizes reasonable values). Like other tools or artifacts, moralities are evaluated by how well they do this job. To the extent that they do it well, they are wise; to the extent that they do it badly, they are foolish.

Because the instrumentalist believes that moral principles may be wise or foolish, but not true or false, intuitions about cases and principles do not count as evidence for or against principles (though they may hint at what makes sense).[8] Rather, we are concerned with whether adopting a principle will promote our reasonable values. Accordingly, instrumental theories are constrained by social realities in ways that at least most metaphysical theories are not.[9] To begin with, instrumental theories must consider the impact of our adopting a principle at expected levels of compliance. We cannot just look for principles that would be best were everyone to comply with them (as some formulations of utilitarianism would have it) or principles that are known to be true by reason. We need to consider the role a principle will actually play in the regulation of social life. This means we must be concerned with the actual likelihood of compliance, the likelihood of abuse, and the consequences of acting on them in a world where others do not. Utopian principles can be interesting and useful to consider, they may show us how far we have fallen or how high beings of our biology may rise, but they do not tell us what principles it makes sense for us now to adopt.

For the instrumentalist, to advocate a moral standard is not to affirm a truth, but rather to take a moral stand in favor of or against a category of action. The instrumentalist's bumper sticker reads "Ethics is Us." To speak of *our* ethics or *our* morality is to speak of the standards of conduct and character to which we hold each other. To argue in favor of a principle prohibiting or requiring a certain kind of conduct is to argue that we should take a strong collective stand for or against that conduct. We take such stands by praising, blaming, and bestowing or withholding optional benefits and burdens (for example, friendship, social inclusion, gifts, cold shoulders).

But if our society does not take a stand with respect to a category of action, or if one believes it has taken the wrong stand, there will be many cases in which one may sincerely advocate a standard without being obligated to act on it. In many cases, a principle that would work well were most people to act on it will work badly if only a few do. In other cases, acting on a principle that would work well given a high level of compliance would be a disaster given low levels of compliance.[10] This idea, of course, stands in sharp contrast to the metaphysical moralist's view. On that view, to sincerely advocate a standard is to assert its truth.

For the instrumentalist, the corresponding point holds in relation to the meanings of contested moral terms (and hence the meanings of our moral principles). Our use of language sets outside boundaries on the meanings of our terms, but disputes about contested terms arise within these boundaries. Thus, language tells us that sexist acts are wrongful gender-related acts, but we may disagree about which particular gender-related acts are sexist. Metaphysical moralists treat this as something to be discovered. Instrumentalists hold that there is no truth about the matter. Rather, it is something we decide. Accordingly, to propose an "analysis" is the same thing as defending a moral standard (or set of moral standards). In effect, it selects certain gender-related behavior to prohibit. Accordingly, moral analyses are justified in the same way moral standards are (that is, by how well they contribute to promoting reasonable values).[11]

Because principles for distributing praise and blame are evaluated in relation to the goal of promoting and protecting reasonably valued ways of life, they are not properly keyed to moral worth (as understood by the metaphysical moralist). The instrumentalist believes that moral worth, as understood by the metaphysical moralist, is a myth. The instrumentalist acknowledges there is a sense in which people have qualities and perform actions that are deserving of praise and blame. But she understands "deserving" in instrumental terms. Again, our principles for praising and blaming are judged by how well they promote and protect a reasonably valued way of life. Accordingly, they may differ from culture to culture, from historical period to historical period, and even from one area of social life to another (compare, e.g., the family, the military, and the therapist). Moral worth is not some quality or property of the will or the soul that can be measured by a set of standards that transcends these differences.

Accordingly, the instrumentalist denies that moral worth necessarily takes precedence over other kinds of worth in our evaluation of persons. We value people for their moral character, but we value them for other things as well. A scrupulously moral person who is also cold, tedious, unimaginative, and as ungenerous as morality allows is not necessarily a better person than a warm, inventive, contagiously happy, humorous, and big-hearted person who breaks a few promises and tells a few lies. According to the instrumentalist, morality can be given too much importance (the name for the excess is "moralism").[12]

Instrumentalism also denies that moral considerations necessarily trump other values, at least as this is understood by the metaphysical moralist. This metaphysical moralist's principle is only as clear as the metaphysical moralist's distinction between moral and nonmoral values. But the spirit of the view is clear enough. We ought never to sacrifice moral principles to increase the happiness of those we love, to make the world more beautiful, to advance knowledge, and so forth. The instrumentalist denies this. Because she believes that moral principles are evaluated in relation to how well they serve other (reasonable) values, morality has no pride of place. Big aesthetic gains may justify minor promise-breaking. Small lies may be justified to escape a tedious evening. The relative importance of moral to what the metaphysical moralist regards as nonmoral considerations is itself determined on instrumental grounds.[13]

Finally, like the metaphysical moralist, the instrumentalist believes that questions about moral principles are asked from an impartial point of view. But the kind of impartiality involved is different. The impartiality of the metaphysical moralist has to do with one's state of mind. The impartiality the instrumentalist favors has to do with the sort of question one is asking and is, in fact, built into the meaning of "morality" itself. The contrasts to "moral" are "prudential" and "partisan." I can ask which standards are worthy of my support from any of these points of view. If I ask it from a prudential point of view, I am asking what standards would be best for me. If I ask it from a partisan point of view, I am asking what standards would be best for some group (e.g., the French). If I ask it from a moral point of view, I am asking what standards would be better for us (i.e., for all parties affected). This requires that I give everyone's interests and everyone's reasonable values equal weight.

The Relation to the Standard Distinctions

As suggested, moral philosophers typically divide ethical theories into two camps, deontic and teleological. Teleological theories defend principles and actions on the basis of their consequences, that is, on the basis of how well they promote goods or diminish evils. So what is the difference between teleological theories and instrumental theories?

A full response to this question must address difficult issues that are beyond the scope of this paper, but enough can be said here for our purposes. To begin with, teleological theories can be either metaphysical or instrumental.

Consider the simplest case, act utilitarianism. Act utilitarian holds that an action is right if and only if it produces the most favorable balance of happiness over unhappiness. An act utilitarian who believes that this principle states a truth binding on rational agents as such, that it takes precedence over all other principles, that it holds unconditionally, and that one's moral worth is a function of the extent to which one honors it is (to that extent) a metaphysical moralist. But an act utilitarian might also reject all this. She might hold instead that moralities are social tools that are justified to the extent that they promote and protect reasonably valued ways of life. She might think that happiness and unhappiness are the only things that reasonably matter here and that we promote the most favorable balance between them by taking a collective stand in favor of the utility principle. If she were convinced that we could do better with respect to reasonable values by shifting to a morality centered around rights, duties, and obligations (or a morality centered around the virtues) she would support that. A metaphysical moralist who subscribes to act utilitarianism could not be so flexible. She believes that act utilitarianism is just plain true, that it is a deliverance of philosophical reason, and that our conformity to it is a measure of our worth as human beings

Teleological theories are distinguished from deontological theories. The expression "deontological theory" is used in two ways. First, a deontologist holds that principles of right and wrong always trump consequences (e.g., that we should not violate the principle "Never punish an innocent person" even to save thousands of lives). If an instrumentalist believed that our taking a collective stand of this kind best promotes a reasonably valued way of life (under prevailing circumstances), he could consistently support such a view. On the other hand, "deontological" is sometimes used to refer to the metaethical position that principles of right and wrong cannot be justified by appealing to the consequences of adopting them. An instrumentalist cannot adopt this kind of deontological theory, but a deontologist of this kind is not necessarily a metaphysical moralist either. He becomes a metaphysical moralist to the extent that he takes these principles to be moral truths binding on rational agents as such, to take precedence over all other principles, to hold unconditionally, to be measures of moral worth, and so forth. I think that most deontologists do in fact subscribe to most such background assumptions, but they hold them qua metaphysical moralist, not qua deontologists.

The Consequences for Humanitarian Intervention

Because instrumentalism and the metaphysical conception are not moral theories—because they are each compatible with any set of action guiding principles—it might seem surprising that they have any implications for our approach to questions of humanitarian intervention at all. In what follows I will describe important differences in at least five areas. Before so doing, however, it should be noted that there is something odd about application of the metaphysical conception to questions of international ethics. After all, the metaphysical conception holds that morality is a measure of moral worth and that moral worth (somehow) resides in (or supervenes on) the will or soul of a rational being. Theorists of international ethics, on the other hand, look for principles to govern the relations between states (which, after all, have nothing like a rational will). Still, many discussions of international ethics treat principles in ways that are informed by the metaphysical conception. This is especially true in relation to discussions of human rights and reparations. Moreover, discussions of principles by which states should govern their mutual relations can be reformulated as questions about the ways that heads of states should act.

How, then, does the difference between these two approaches to morality influence our approach to questions of international ethics in general and humanitarian intervention in particular?

To begin with, the instrumentalist endorses those standards for international ethics that she thinks would best serve all parties affected at the expected levels of compliance. She must consider, among other things, the extent to which a principle might destabilize the international system, the extent to which a principle might function as a smokescreen behind which powerful nations bully less powerful nations to their own ends, and the extent to which the standard would deter governments from abusing their citizens in the long run. Accordingly, the principles she endorses will depend importantly on her understanding of how the world works.

The same can not be said of metaphysical moralists. The principles they seek are thought to be discoverable by reason. Intuitionists believe we can find those truths by reflecting on cases or principles. Because they are looking for general principles governing states (or collections of rational agents), as such, they are free and even obliged to consult intuitions set in hypothetical (possible) worlds. In fact, cases set in hypothetical worlds may be preferable since they do not provoke partisan sentiments or emotional attachments. Moreover, these cases need not involve states at all. Thus, for example, if the question is whether we should send troops into an area to save the lives of citizens threatened by militias, an intuitionist might focus on well-known cases from the literature of killing and letting die (e.g., trolley cases).[14] The result is a neglect of how the world actually works.

Respect for persons based on metaphysical theories have this feature as well. They attempt to determine the content of morality by considering what it is to respect rational agents as such.[15] There are many different ways to understand this, but none of them require one to think seriously about how the world actually works. Rational agency is the same in all times and places. Respect for rational agency is also the same. Discussions of these matters might focus on the rights human beings have as rational agents (i.e., human rights) and on the obligations human beings have to others whose rights have been or are being violated. Of course, empirical considerations are relevant when it comes to applying the principles generated by these discussions. However, to the extent one is a metaphysical moralist, they are not relevant to arriving at the principles themselves.

This means that metaphysical moralists typically will not concern themselves with the sort of challenges posed by the realist school of international relations. It does not matter to their analysis whether the principles typically advanced to support or oppose interventions can be and often are smokescreens behind which powerful states exploit or otherwise mistreat less powerful states to their own selfish ends. It does not matter that no state can reasonably be expected to constrain its pursuit of its good to act morally. It is not a defect of a principle that states ignore or abuse it, it is a defect of the states. The philosopher's job is to discover the principle and let the chips fall where they may. Again, if the principle is true, it binds unconditionally. It does not matter what others do or are likely to do.

The challenge of the realist school, however, must be taken seriously by instrumentalists. If moral considerations could not in any way influence the behavior of states in relation to each other (now or in the future), there would be no point looking for principles. Part of the problem facing any instrumentalist theory is to determine when and how moral principles could be effective. This will constrain the range of principles it makes sense to consider. Suppose, for example, one believes that principles requiring or restricting humanitarian intervention can influence the behavior of states only in cases they regard as borderline or nearly borderline with respect to their interests. And suppose one believes that these principles can operate in such cases because they can mobilize grassroots popular sentiment. In that case, one would want to frame principles that can effectively mobilize popular sentiment. As I will argue presently, this consideration may determine whether the instrumentalist should accept or reject principles stated in the language of human rights.

These differences in how moral and instrumental theorists arrive at principles affect the attitudes they may reasonably adopt in relation to those principles, especially with respect to questions of negotiation and compromise. The reasonable instrumentalist will be much more of a fallibilist. After all, the empirical questions in relation to which he defends his principles are often very complicated and highly undetermined by the evidence. His position on these questions is often based on general views about how the world works for which he has no real proof. Our differences frequently reflect the fact that we trust different information sources. They may also reflect different interpretations of historical events, particularly in relation to the motives and intentions of political leaders. That is, they may involve what John Rawls calls conjecture and speculation. Because instrumentalists must acknowledge this, they also acknowledge that there is plenty of room for reasonable people to disagree about principles. For this reason, instrumentalists are (or should be) open to compromise and negotiation both with respect to principles and with respect to their application in particular cases.

Metaphysical theorists, on the other hand, believe that reason delivers the truth about these matters. They are also trained to believe that they are entitled to trust their own intuitions and inferences (even where these conflict with other philosophers). This bit of professionally licensed hubris entitles metaphysical moralists to take the deliverances of their own reason as the truth of the matter. This makes negotiation and compromise a much less desirable alternative for them. If one is convinced that his position is demanded by morality, to compromise is to be willing to have the matter settled at the expense of morality. This is especially difficult for the metaphysical moralist since moral considerations are supposed to be supreme. In this regard, the situation of the metaphysical moralists is comparable to that of the religious moralist.

Relatedly, since the metaphysical moralist believes that moral standards are supreme, she also believes that we must act on them even at great risk or sacrifice to ourselves. If a metaphysical moralist believes that it is wrong for states to fight wars, she must oppose her own state fighting a war even in self-defense. If she believes it is the obligation of prosperous nations to feed the starving in impoverished nations, she must urge her own state to do this even if that means significantly sacrificing its own prosperity. If she thinks it is morally obligatory to intervene in the affairs of other states to stop widespread human rights abuses, she must favor intervention even if it involves great risk to her own population (e.g., through terrorist reprisals).

Instrumentalist theories do not have this feature. Instrumentalists may argue that moral principles are not taken seriously enough or given enough weight by states. That is, they might think that the community of states (or their populations) would be better off—from an impartial point of view—if they gave moral considerations greater weight. Nonetheless, they do not think that moral standards necessarily take precedence over all other considerations. Accordingly, they might favor violating a moral standard on some occasion to achieve an important end or avoid a serious risk. That is, they might favor what is ordinarily called "being practical" on certain occasions.

Because the metaphysical theorist believes her reason delivers moral truths that bind unconditionally, she cannot sincerely endorse a principle without also advocating that states act on that principle. In particular, she can not hold "P is true, but since not enough states follow P, we are not obligated to do so either." For her, this would be like saying that the principle prohibiting cruelty would be true only if a sufficient number of people were not cruel. Of course, a metaphysical moralist can endorse policies as moral only on the condition that others do the same (e.g., disarmament), but these policies or low level principles must be defended in relation to moral principles that are true and hold unconditionally.

From an instrumentalist standpoint, this is a serious disadvantage. After all, some principles might be foolish to adopt because no one now acts on them, but would make sense to adopt were enough other states to do the same (e.g., it is wrong for democratic states to manipulate the internal politics of other democratic states). The instrumentalist is free to endorse such principles—to argue that it would be best were all relevant states to adopt them—without insisting that his or any other state ought to act on them now. A metaphysical moralist will hold that if this principle is true, one must act on it whether others do or not.

Another important difference concerns the shape of the theory of intervention itself. Because the instrumentalist approaches conceptual issues differently than the metaphysical moralist, he will approach the issue of intervention with a different methodology. The metaphysical moralist will begin her inquiries with questions about the rights of sovereign nations and the conditions under which they may be infringed (or forfeited). This naturally leads to questions like: what is autonomy, really? what is self-determination, really? what is legitimacy really? what is the true nature and basis of sovereignty? and what exactly are the rights of sovereign nations?

The instrumentalist does not believe that we can discover the answer to these questions. Rather, these are matters we decide. Within the outside constraints imposed by language, he will attempt to fix the meanings of these central terms in the ways that get what he takes to be the best set of principles. Roughly, "intervention" is defined in English as the imposition of one's will on a state in matters that would ordinarily be thought to fall within the rights of that state as a sovereign nation. So, before we know what counts as an intervention we need an account, for example, of the rights of sovereign nations. For the instrumentalist this is not something we discover, but something we decide. In fact, the problem of intervention is importantly a problem of deciding what set of rights would best serve the society of states (from an impartial point of view).

For the instrumentalist, the real question is what forms of influence (including force) states legitimately may impose on other states and under what conditions. Instead of thinking about what "intervention" really means, the instrumentalist will think about the various types of influence states can exert on each other and the conditions (if any) under which each type of influence is justified. At one end of the continuum are relatively mild prods like diplomatic rebukes. At the other end are full scale military invasions intended to overthrow a government. In the middle, there are trade penalties, embassy closures, blockades and embargoes, financial support to opposition parties, assassinations, limited military assaults, economic sabotage, and other covert actions aimed to destabilize or overturn a government. The instrumentalist seeks principles covering all these matters that make the most sense from an impartial point of view.

Finally, I want to contrast the metaphysical conception and the instrumentalist conception on the important issue of human rights. The metaphysical moralist believes that human rights can be important to this discussion only in the case that she believes that there are such things as human rights. If she believes there are human rights and that human rights violations are serious matters, she will need to decide under what conditions, if any, human rights violations justify intervention. To do this she needs to answer three sets of questions:

1. What count as violations of human rights (for example, does severe poverty count? Does censorship of artistic expression? Does lack of economic opportunity? What about widespread illiteracy? Does famine count? What about disease that could be eliminated by a program of affordable vaccinations?).

2. What agents must be responsible for these violations to justify intervention? Must governments be direct causal agents? Is it enough that a government does nothing to eliminate features of a social or economic system that promote these violations?

3. What follows from the fact that human rights have been violated by the appropriate agents? In particular, does this create a right to intervene or a duty to intervene or sometimes one and sometimes the other, depending on their severity? And for whom does it create this right or this duty?

Metaphysical moralists believe that there is a truth about these matters that is discoverable by the moral epistemology sketched earlier. One of the reasons the question of humanitarian intervention is so difficult for them is that they have such a difficult time generating any significant agreement on these issues. There is not even a consensus on what count as human rights to begin with.

Instrumentalists may, if they wish, appeal to human rights. This is not because they believe reason tells us there are such rights, but rather because they believe that attributing human rights to us helps provide us with important protections that contribute to promoting reasonable values. They may also believe that the language of human rights has such moral currency that to refuse to talk in these terms is to marginalize oneself. Of course, such an instrumentalist will rely on instrumental considerations to decide what counts as human rights, what follows from their violation, and so forth.

On the other hand, an instrumentalist is free to reject the idea of human rights. She might want to do so, for example, if she favors interventions to prevent widespread murder, rape, and torture. She might believe that the rhetoric of human rights only very weakly expresses her reasons for wanting to intervene. After all, to describe unbridled brutality as a violation of human rights is to assimilate it to government suppression of free speech or to limitations on voting rights. No one seriously argues for military intervention (or any serious interventions at all) for these reasons, and yet voting rights and free speech are (on some lists) among the most important human rights. This assimilation, then, may weaken the rhetorical case for invading another country to prevent widespread murder, torture, famine, and so forth. If we want our principles to mobilize local constituencies to support intervention in these cases, we should support a principle that permits intervention to prevent murder, rape, torture, and genocide. To describe these as human rights violations is highly euphemistic and unlikely to mobilize sufficient support to bring about an intervention.

Illustrations

It might help to clarify these issues by providing brief sketches of instrumental and metaphysical arguments for and against intervention. To simplify, let us consider one of the worst-case scenarios. An autocratic government serving an economic elite is committing widespread murder and torture against a particular segment of its population to bolster its power and/or increase its wealth. How should the society of states respond to such cases? Under what conditions should our international ethic permit or require military intervention?

THE INSTRUMENTALIST ARGUMENT

The instrumentalist argument needs a principle that best serves all populations affected from an impartial point of view. [16] These populations include those vulnerable to abuse (now and in the future), those who profit from the abuse, and those likely to be affected by interventions (by standing by and doing nothing). Of course, there are many competing principles for generating tradeoffs between the aggregation and distribution of benefits and burdens across a collection of persons such that the collection is better off as a whole. But I do not need to choose a particular principle to make my case here. The candidates for murder and torture are far more numerous than the elites, now and in any foreseeable future. The benefits reaped by the elites could not possibly balance the suffering inflicted by their murder and torture. The populations of states everywhere would obviously be better off under policies that rendered elites somewhat less wealthy and secure but better protected vulnerable people against murder and torture. If you doubt this, suppose you had to choose between living in a world in which elites are free to murder and torture and a world in which they were prevented from doing so, without knowing to which group you would belong (i.e., behind Rawls's veil of ignorance). Suppose your identity in that world would be decided by a chance mechanism sensitive to the population sizes. Would you not choose the world without the murder and torture? If God were to intervene surgically to stop the murder and torture, who could think the world worse off by it (considering the matter impartially)?

I would have no qualms about intervention in such cases were God to do it. But God does not, states do, and states can't be trusted. First, powerful states will abuse any principle we formulate to bully less powerful states to their own ends, undermining self-determination. Second, military interventions will almost always cause disproportionate suffering to innocent people (including the members of the intervening armies). Third, the state system is a fragile thing. Interventions are almost certain to destabilize it and raise the likelihood of war. Finally, given the dismal intelligence-gathering record of organizations like the CIA and the vulnerability of the intervention process to local political pressures, the prospects for intelligent interventions that achieve their objectives are dim. Big mistakes are guaranteed. In some cases, we will intervene on the wrong side. In other cases, we will intervene clumsily and unsuccessfully. We are at least as likely to make things significantly worse as we are to make them significantly better.

The instrumentalist who favors intervention might reply as follows. Powerful states will intervene in the affairs of less powerful states whenever they believe it is clearly in their interest to do so. A principle permitting humanitarian intervention is unlikely to make that happen any more often than it already does. The most we can expect from a state's commitment to a principle mandating intervention is that it will be more likely to intervene in cases that are borderline or nearly borderline with respect to its interests, because commitment to the principle will give local constituencies that favor intervention an organizing tool. Given the political risks involved, these authentically humanitarian interventions are not likely to be undertaken unless a government is reasonably certain that they can be carried out without much loss of life (as happened, for example, in Haiti). Again, since powerful states frequently intervene in the affairs of less powerful states, these interventions will not introduce anything new into the state system and will not seriously destabilize it. The risk of unintelligent and misinformed humanitarian intervention is real but not great. After all, we can expect states to move cautiously and reluctantly when it comes to spending money and risking lives for merely moral reasons. Without intervention and the threat of intervention, however, it is certain that autocratic national elites will murder and torture on a massive scale. From an impartial point of view, the benefits obviously outweigh the risks.

I am not going to develop the argument further. Enough has been said to show that the issues dividing instrumentalists on this issue are almost entirely empirical. Let us contrast this to how a metaphysical moralist proceeds.

THE METAPHYSICAL MORALIST ARGUMENT

All rational beings have a right to self-determination. That is obvious. The sovereignty of states is justified only if it protects a people's right to collective self-determination. Whatever our final analysis of that right, it is clear that an autocratic government that serves only an elite violates it. Such a government lacks authority and legitimacy. Other governments have no moral obligation to respect it. Neither do private citizens.

As our intuitions in scores of cases central to the literature of killing and letting die establish, there is a strong moral obligation to rescue (Rachels' bathtub case may even establish that it is as strong as the obligation not to murder itself).[17] Accordingly, if we are in a position to do so, we must defend helpless people against murderers (whether the murderers are government agents or private citizens). Not to do so when we are in a position to do so is as bad (or nearly so) as killing those people ourselves. Those who do not share these intuitions just want to look the other way. They are preoccupied with their own selfish concerns, so they make no genuine effort vividly to imagine the slaughter. Those who know what it is like to be among the slaughtered also know that something must be done.

Of course, military intervention can be risky. We put our soldiers in jeopardy, and we invite reprisals. But moral considerations always take precedence over considerations of self-interest. We must choose between doing what we know to be right and protecting the hides of our own citizens, including our own hides. It is the choice that Humphrey Bogart faced at the end of *Casablanca*. We know he chose well.

Of course, governments may abuse principles justifying intervention. We cannot help that, but it should not stop us from articulating principles we know to be true and urging governments to adopt them. Otherwise, we are simply complicit in their evil. The fact that we live in a corrupt world is no excuse for being corrupt ourselves.

A sketch of a metaphysical moralist's argument against intervention might run as follows. Military intervention will almost certainly cause harm and death to some innocent persons in every case. It is a self-evident truth that it is always wrong to harm the innocent, a truth further established by our responses to countless "punish the innocent" counter-examples to utilitarianism and by the vast literature on "trolley cases."[18] Of course it is good to protect people against evil, but not at the cost of doing evil oneself. Morality forbids us to play the numbers game (something we also know from the trolley cases). A life is a life. No matter how you try to disguise it, killing an innocent person is murder, and murder is morally intolerable. It does not matter that our intention in dropping our bombs is to protect innocents, not to kill them. If we know in advance that dropping our bombs will kill innocents, we have murdered them. This is clear from an analysis of the concept of "murder" and from our intuitions in many well-known cases in the literature on the doctrine of double effect.

It is clear that this discussion has little or no empirical content. What is right is "discovered" by appealing to intuitions about cases and principles. Once that is known, we do not need to inquire further about expected levels of compliance, the probability of abuse, the costs and risks of acting on principles when most other states do not, and so forth.

Evaluation

I want to conclude briefly by discussing the strengths and weaknesses of each conception.

The metaphysical conception has two big problems. The first is immediately recognized by most beginning students of ethics. In the face of all the historical, cultural, and individual diversity in moral judgments and principles, how can one claim that there is one true "Morality," knowable to all rational beings? Defenders of the metaphysical conception have developed many ingenious responses to this objection. Philosophers are still debating the issue. For those who are interested, I discuss these responses at length in Chapter 1 of *Between Universalism and Skepticism* (Oxford University Press, 1994) and conclude that none of them succeed.

The second problem concerns the idea of moral worth. The metaphysical moralist understands moral worth as a feature of our soul or will. For many reasons, the instrumentalist believes that this idea lacks content, since we have no real way to measure our own moral worth or the moral worth of others. Suppose, for example, that someone does something terrible, believing sincerely that he does something right (e.g., participates in ethnic cleansing). For what exactly is his moral worth reduced? We cannot say it is reduced by virtue of the transition between his belief and his action. No one is to be blamed for doing what he thinks is right, as such. If there is reduced moral worth, it resides in his beliefs themselves, or rather, how he came to hold and keep them. On the most plausible version, he is blamed for not putting as much (or the right kind of) effort or energy into his beliefs as he should. But how much do we blame him for that? As much as for participating in ethnic cleansing? What if he has devoted considerable time and attention to arriving at his views? What if he is not particularly bright and simply trusted the judgment of those he identified as the intelligent people in his community? What if believing that ethnic cleansing is wrong would earn him the contempt of his friends and family? In general, how much and what kind of effort, energy, and sacrifice can we legitimately expect from someone in the area of belief formation and retention?

We have no clear answers to these questions. The ethics of belief is a woefully underdeveloped area in philosophy and for good reason. We really do not know enough about the psychology of belief to develop it, and it is difficult to anticipate advances in psychology that will enable us to do so. No explanations of belief formation and retention generated by psychologists are likely directly to concern themselves with questions of effort and energy relevant to assessing moral worth, so we have no way of assessing moral worth in these cases.

Corresponding considerations arise in relation to the other kind of wrongdoing, such as intentionally doing wrong (i.e., doing wrong believing that it is wrong). I cannot consider these matters in any detail here, but this much can be said. Perhaps the most important subset of these cases are cases of weakness of the will. Philosophers since Aristotle have been trying to explain the very possibility of this phenomenon and have yet to converge on a doctrine. Nothing that has been said, moreover, will help us to assess degrees of weakness or will otherwise help us determine how much moral worth one loses for particular acts of weakness.

If we reject the metaphysical idea of moral worth, we have little or no reason to subscribe to the supremacy of the moral or the idea that moral standards bind unconditionally.

The metaphysical moralist also has serious complaints against the instrumentalist. To begin with, instrumentalism seems to reduce morality to just another mechanism of social control. For this reason, it cannot explain the special role morality rightly has in our lives. Nor can it provide a convincing answer to the question "Why be moral?" How is the instrumentalist to respond to one who says, "I'm happy that the rest of these people are moral. That makes my life easier. But I see no reason why I should be." There seems to be something fundamentally wrong with that response, and only the metaphysical moralist can explain it.

Relatedly, instrumentalism conflicts with our deep intuitive sense that moral worth is not just a social construct. The basis of moral worth may be difficult to describe in a philosophically satisfying way, but we know that people who practice brutality, betrayal, selfishness, bullying, cheating, and so forth are defective human beings in a very particular way (in a way that differs, for example, from people who are slow-witted or bad athletes). What they lack, quite clearly, is moral worth.

There is something strange about the instrumentalist theory of praising and blaming, for the instrumentalist makes the same judgments as the rest of us when she is victimized. She blames, and her blame is not just a judgment to the effect that her persecutor violated some principle that supports a reasonably valued way of life. It is far more personal than that. It is a judgment of the person himself, not a judgment of the relation of his act to some social rule. An instrumentalist might try to accommodate this to her theory by holding that we should blame in a personal way for instrumental reasons. But since she denies that there is such a thing as moral worth, to argue we should blame in this way is to argue that we should act as if some myth were true. Thus, if she has any integrity, she must urge us to stop blaming in this personal way, although it is obvious to us that this kind of blame is justified.

Finally, it might be argued, just as the metaphysical moralist has difficulty explicating the central idea of moral worth, the instrumentalist has difficulty explicating the central notions of "reasonable values" and "an impartial point of view." What exactly are "reasonable values"? Several theories of value are open to an instrumentalist, but there is no consensus in favor of any of them.[19]

Furthermore, there is no consensus on what it means for a principle to count everyone's interests equally. In fact, as the mountains of literature on Rawls's early work establishes, there is no uniquely rational way to do this.

As an instrumentalist, I believe there are satisfactory answers to these complaints, and I believe I have made them elsewhere. My purpose in this chapter, however, is simply to show how these two approaches to moral philosophy affect our approach to the question of humanitarian intervention and to give you a sense of the strengths and weaknesses of these approaches.

Notes

1. G.E.M. Anscombe, "Modern Moral Philosophy," *Ethics, Religion, and Politics*, Vol. 3 (1958; Minneapolis: University of Minnesota Press, 1981) Chapter 4.

2. This claim is ambiguous in a way that is rarely recognized. It could mean that moral considerations take precedence over all other considerations when we are deciding the morally right thing to do. Or it could mean that the morally right thing to do always trumps considerations of other kinds in deciding how to act. The first interpretation is compatible with the claim that nonmoral considerations may sometimes trump moral considerations when we decide what we ought to do, all things considered. The second is compatible with the claim that nonmoral considerations may trump moral considerations in determining the morally right thing to do. To endorse the supremacy of the moral in a strong sense, one needs to accept the supremacy of the moral in both of these senses. It turns out, however, that this conjunction is very implausible. For a detailed discussion of these matters see my paper "Moralism and the Good," *Philosophical Studies* 52.1 (July 1987).

3. Alan Gewirth, *Reason and Morality* (Chicago, IL: The University of Chicago Press, 1978) 1.

4. D.Z. Philips, "In Search of the Moral Must," *Philosophical Quarterly* 27.107 (April 1977) 150.

5. Susan Wolf, "Moral Saints," *The Journal of Philosophy* 79 (August 1982).

6. See, for example, Baruch Brodie, "Intuitions and Objective Moral Knowledge," *Monist* 62 (October 1979); and M.B.E. Smith, "Ethical Intuitionism and Naturalism: A Reconciliation," *The Canadian Journal of Philosophy*, 9.4 (1979). Smith's paper was recommended to me in conversation by John Rawls as the single best defense of intuitionism of which he was aware. Rawls himself relied importantly (though not exclusively) on intuitions to establish or test moral principles in his most famous work, *A Theory of Justice* (Cambridge, MA: Harvard University Press, 1972). He does not make much use of them in his later work, however. Norman Daniels takes intuitions to be one kind of evidence of objective moral truth (though not the only kind) in a series of papers defending a method he calls "wide reflective equilibrium" (which he describes as a reformulation of Rawlsean ideas). The best known of these papers is "Wide Reflective Equilibrium and Theory Acceptance in Ethics," *Journal of Philosophy* 76 (1979). For a critique of intuitionism, see Chapter 1 of my book, *Between Universalism and Skepticism* (Oxford: Oxford University Press, 1994).

7. For an interesting and sustained attempt to do this, see Alan Donagan, *The Theory of Morality* (Chicago, IL: University of Chicago Press, 1977). The principle that persons ought be respected is widespread in English language philosophy, although many of its defenders do not try to derive any very specific principles of morality from it. In many cases, to respect persons seems to amount to little more than taking their interests into account in ones actions; see, e.g., David Gautier, *Practical Reasoning* (Oxford: Oxford University Press, 1963) 119. In other cases, it seems to amount to little more than respecting morality itself; see, e.g., B.J. Diggs, "A Contractarian View of Respect for Persons," *American Philosophical Quarterly* 18.4 (1981): 276. For a critique of these attempts, see Chapter 1 of *Between Universalism and Skepticism*.

8. Not all metaphysical moralists would describe moral principles as true or false. One could hold with Kant and Hare that moral principles are imperatives. However, this does not affect the spirit of the position or its difference from the instrumentalist view, since a metaphysical moralist who held this view would nonetheless insist that it is true that morality consists of some particular set of imperatives and that these imperatives tell us how we must act to achieve moral worth.

9. Utilitarians, of course, are constrained by social realities. As suggested, one can adopt utilitarianism (of any variety) as an instrumental theory or a metaphysical theory. One holds it as a metaphysical theory to the extent that one believes that it describes a universal moral truth, that it is known by intuition, that our moral worth depends on the degree to which we

conform to it, that it takes precedence over all other principles in deciding how we ought to act, all things considered, and so forth. An instrumentalist, of course, rejects all of this. She will be a utilitarian (of whatever variety) if she holds that we best promote and defend a reasonably valued way of life by adopting that variety of utilitarianism as our social morality.

10. See my paper "Thoughts on the Transition from Ideal to nonIdeal Theory," *Nous* 19.9 (1985).

11. I argue for this in "The Myth of Moral Analysis" (circulating).

12. See my paper "Moralism and the Good," *Philosophical Studies* 52.1 (1987), and Susan Wolfe's paper "Moral Saints" (note 5).

13. The instrumentalist, however, is free to treat moral values as worth realizing for their own sake. That is, for example, she is free to treat justice as something we ought to value intrinsically. Her reason for doing this is instrumental. By treating justice in this way, we best promote our system of reasonable values. To say that we should value something intrinsically (on this view) is not to say that it really has intrinsic value but only that it is good for us (given who we are) to adopt a certain attitude toward it (such as, the attitude that it is worth pursuing for its own sake). For a detailed defense and account of these views, see Chapters 5 and 6 of my *Between Universalism and Skepticism*.

14. The trolley case goes as follows: a trolley is hurtling out of control down a track on which several people are standing, oblivious to its approach. You are passing by and have a chance to throw a switch, diverting the trolley on to another track and so saving the people. However, there is a woman on the other track. The question is whether one should take one life in order to save several.

15. By respect for persons theories I have in mind theories that derive the content of morality from the principle that persons must be respected. (See note 7.)

16. It is not obvious how to do this. Deciding what best serves a population from an impartial point of view requires that we take into account both the amounts of the goods and evils at stake and the distribution of these goods and evils. As I argue in Chapter 4 of *Between Universalism and Skepticism*, there is no uniquely rational way to do this.

17. See James Rachels, "Active and Passive Euthanasia," *The New England Journal of Medicine* 292 (9 January 1975). For a response to this approach, see my paper "Weighing Moral Reasons," *Mind* 96 (July 1987) and Chapter 4 of *Between Universalism and Skepticism*.

18. Utilitarianism is standardly criticized on the ground that it would require us to punish (e.g., jail or execute) people we know to be innocent in order to promote the greater good. For a response to this criticism see my paper "The Inevitability of Punishing the Innocent," *Philosophical Studies* 48.4 (1985).

19. For my version of this, see Chapters 5 and 6 of my *Between Universalism and Skepticism*. Perhaps the most popular theories identify the good as preference satisfaction (or the satisfaction of rational desires). I argue against this in Chapter 3 of *Between Universalism and Skepticism*.

5

Preempting Humanitarian Interventions

Thomas Pogge

Let me define humanitarian intervention, roughly, as coercive external interference in the internal affairs of a sovereign state justified by the goal of protecting large numbers of persons within this state in the enjoyment of their human rights. In most cases, the massive human-rights problems that provide reasons for humanitarian interventions are due to those who hold, or try to gain, power in the foreign state in question. What follows will implicitly have this central case in mind, though I recognize that there are other cases, such as natural calamities or the collapse of governmental authority.

Normative discussions of humanitarian intervention often focus on the question whether some particular actual or hypothetical intervention is good or bad, whether it may or should be undertaken or not. Such discussions then give rise to a more general examination of what moral criteria might be suitable for answering questions of the first type in a principled way.

These discussions are important, but resting content with them is myopic by failing to acknowledge that *all* humanitarian interventions are bad in a sense, that it would be best if the world could get along without them. This is not to say that there is anything wrong with the existence of humanitarian intervention as an available response to serious human-rights problems. But we should want—partly through the availability of this option perhaps—to avoid situations that call for its exercise. We should want to avoid humanitarian interventions both because it is bad for there to be the kind of massive human-rights problems that furnish reasons to intervene in the first place and also because, due to their coercive nature, such interventions themselves usually cause, or at least risk, human-rights problems of their own, even when they are beneficial on the whole.

Put in so abstract a way, the point can hardly be disputed. Yes, other things equal, it is indeed a worthy goal to reduce or eliminate the situations that provide reasons for humanitarian interventions. The interesting questions are whose goal exactly is this supposed to be and how exactly is this goal to be pursued?

Let me distinguish four approaches defined by how they respond to this pair of questions. The first is *preventive diplomacy*. It assigns the worthy goal to the foreign policy establishment of a certain noble superpower and instructs these experts to conduct its foreign policy with this goal in mind. Taking the world as it is, they are to exert the influence of the US in support of human rights abroad. There is little more that can be said in general terms by way of specifying that instruction. This is so because of the need for flexibility, which arises from the triple complexity of diplomacy—there is, first, the complexity of facts. To act effectively with regard to some particular foreign country, our experts must proceed with a rich and contextualized knowledge of the local circumstances and possibilities. They must know about the personalities, aims, and values of the persons holding or plausibly seeking political or economic power; about their options and opportunities; about the major groups in the country in question as well as their histories, values, and internal organization; about the relations such persons and groups have with third parties abroad and the influences they are subject to on account of such relations—and so on and so forth without limit. A foreign policy expert can never know enough details.

There is, secondly, the complexity of ends. The prevention of human-rights problems abroad is at best only one among many goals of our foreign policy. Here it may be objected that, to the contrary, foreign policy has, or should have, only one such goal: the pursuit of our national interest. There is, however, no widely accepted and clear-cut explication of this expression that would allow us, on purely empirical grounds, to identify and to weight candidate foreign policy goals by reference to their importance to the national interest.[1] Appeal to the national interest then cannot settle debates about how to balance the many candidate ends of foreign policy—for example, about whether and how much to discount the future or about how to trade off concerns about global resource depletion, human rights, the risk of nuclear war, and our share of the global economy.

There is, thirdly, the complexity of means. These are truly endless, as becomes clear by reflecting simply on the ways one person can try to influence the conduct of another: directly, through rewards and punishments, offers and threats, providing and withholding of information and misinformation, etc., or indirectly, by influencing the ways in which third parties influence the target person. If the goal is to influence the policies of, or conditions in, a foreign country, these possibilities grow exponentially.

These rudimentary reflections on the triple complexity of diplomacy show that preventive diplomacy, like diplomacy more generally, is more of an art than a science, at least for persons with merely human brains.

These reflections also begin to reveal the main disadvantage of preventive diplomacy as a method for pursuing the goal of reducing and preempting human-rights problems. Diplomacy deals with incipient human-rights problems in a future-oriented way and on a case-by-case basis, taking full account of the relevant context and the full panoply of our foreign policy goals. Both of these features lend it flexibility, but both of them also make it vulnerable to strategic manipulation. Regarding its contextualized future-orientation, we can appreciate this point through a simple example: suppose we see a human-rights problem emerging in a foreign country and find that its present government is largely responsible for this. We are able to weaken this government in a number of ways, thereby making it more likely that it will be displaced by another. Insofar as we are concerned to promote human rights, we will take this course if and only if we believe that the potential successor government will do better in human-rights terms than the present government. Assuming that the present government understands that this is our criterion, it has an incentive to eliminate any moderate opposition so as to ensure that the only viable alternatives to itself are ones that are even worse. In this way, our known disposition to promote human rights may in fact aggravate human-rights problems abroad—in this case by encouraging the elimination of the present government's more moderate opponents.[2]

Similar considerations hold for the second feature of diplomacy, which is that, when considering the myriad ways of exerting influence abroad, diplomacy ideally takes into account not only the human-rights effects of such exertions, but also their costs and benefits in terms of all our other foreign-policy goals as well. Our foreign policy establishment seeks to maintain and enhance our credibility abroad, to have good relations with foreign governments and other organizations, to support our economic interests, to prevent the spread of dangerous technologies, to reduce global pollution, to enhance public support for our current government at home and abroad, and so on and so forth. Assuming that foreigners understand that we care about all these goals, they can discourage any human-rights promoting policy on our part by increasing its relative cost in terms of our other goals. They can, for example, reward us in various ways for ignoring human-rights problems in their country: They can buy more of our products, support our interests in the UN, reinforce our policies toward third parties, or enhance our government's popularity here or abroad. Equivalently, they can attach various penalties to our attempts to promote human rights in their country. In both of these ways, then, the very flexibility and sensitivity to detail, which are the pride of the art of diplomacy, are also its Achilles heel. They make preventive diplomacy *predictable in the wrong way*, putting foreign governments on notice that they can get away with perpetuating or ignoring their human-rights problems if instead they eliminate plausible alternatives to their rule or establish a negative correlation between our human-rights goal and our other foreign-policy goals. In my view, this mutuality of manipulation in the diplomatic arena is often overlooked by popular commentators (though surely not by true professionals). Our attention is always focused on how *we* are trying to influence *them* in the service of some objective, and rarely is it asked how *they* are trying to influence *us* and, in particular, are trying to influence our attempts to influence them.[3]

These difficulties in the first approach suggest a second, that of a *principled foreign policy* or *PFP*. The word "principled" here stands in contrast to the two sources of flexibility in the *preventive-diplomacy* approach. First, rather than seeking the best response to a particular situation, PFP seeks the best rules or principles for responding to situations of a certain type and then follows these principles even when doing so is not best in a particular case. One such principle might be that we are not going to support a regime under which gross violations of human rights occur, even if its only viable alternative would be even worse, lest we encourage unscrupulous governments to eliminate their more moderate opposition. This point is familiar from many other contexts, ranging from dealing with kidnappers and hijackers to the principles of threat-fulfilling and threat-ignoring in nuclear deterrence.[4] Second, rather than view human rights as one foreign-policy goal among others, PFP views them, to some extent at least, as trumps or side constraints. Thus, we might categorically refuse to support repressive governments through arms sales, no matter how much we may stand to gain in terms of our other goals. The main justification for being principled in these two ways is that this makes our foreign policy predictable in the right way: foreigners are put on notice that they will not be able to manipulate us and that it is therefore pointless for them to try to arrange things so that it would be best for us, in light of our goals, to do what they want us to do.

The main difficulties with the PFP approach are well-known: it is hard for a democracy to commit itself to principles and make this commitment stick. This is so not only because the costs and opportunity costs of sticking to a principle may be high, but also because an election may bring in a different foreign-policy crew (as happened quite dramatically after Ronald Reagan's 1980 defeat of Jimmy Carter). There is the further problem of how principles can cope with the fact that foreign states differ enormously in power and geopolitical importance. Principles that ignore such differentials will demand too little from us in our relations with weak countries or will prove implausibly costly in our relations with strong ones (e.g., by demanding humanitarian intervention in China). And principles that take such power differentials into account are bound to seem hypocritical, as indeed Carter's foreign policy appeared to many (why are human rights of Chinese worth less than those of Haitians?).

In the real world, foreign policy tends to oscillate between these two poles of preventive diplomacy and PFP, though it is usually closer to the pure diplomacy than to the pure principle end of the spectrum. The reason for this may well be that the diplomacy approach allows politicians more leeway for dissimulation: Almost any foreign policy toward China can be presented as one that earnestly seeks to promote human rights through constructive engagement. The announcement of a principled foreign policy guided by human rights, by contrast, imposes real constraints on what decisions can be justified as compatible with these principles.

I do not think there is any general solution to the question where foreign policy should settle on the multi-dimensional diplomacy-principle spectrum. It is easy to say, of course, that we should choose the point that makes our foreign policy most effective in terms of the goals we have assigned to it. But this point is bound to move around with shifts in personnel on the international stage and with changes in many other factors (such as technologies and the distribution of military and economic power). Moreover, this point of maximum effectiveness is impossibly hard to find as the global benefits of commitment to principle cannot be identified, let alone be quantified. We cannot identify or quantify the human-rights problems that would have occurred had we taken a more or less principled stance than we did. So we cannot really know what sort of foreign policy is best—nor can we know how much worse we did than we might have done in a best-case scenario.

What we do know, in general terms, is that the human-rights situation in most countries remains rather bleak even while most of the world's powerful states claim a commitment to human rights as among their foremost foreign-policy goals. And this knowledge provides an impetus to seek and explore alternative approaches.

The two approaches discussed so far differ on how to pursue the goal of reducing or eliminating the situations that provide reasons for humanitarian interventions. But they agree on whose goal this is supposed to be. Both single out, as the main independent variable affecting the overall level of human-rights fulfillment, the ways in which the major democracies conduct their foreign policy.

One main alternative to this shared focus is to identify as the main independent variable the framework of international laws, treaties, and conventions within which governments and other powerful agents interact. Once we assign the goal of promoting human rights to these international "rules of the game," we again face two possibilities. The third approach of *local institutional reform* has recently been illustrated by the proposal of treaties through which small countries would pre-authorize military interventions against themselves for the event that a future government significantly violates democratic principles (Tom Farer) or human rights (Stanley Hoffmann).[5] The point of such treaty pre-authorizations would be not merely to make it easier for outsiders to organize a humanitarian intervention when one seems necessary, but also to hinder the emergence of such serious human-rights problems in the first place. In this respect, pre-authorizing a humanitarian intervention against oneself is akin to anti-takeover measures in the business world, such as poison pills and golden parachutes: predators are less likely to strike as the expected pay-off associated with victory is reduced. The predators whom Farer and Hoffmann are seeking to deter are persons and groups disposed toward taking power by force or toward repressive rule.

Once we begin thinking along these lines, similar anti-takeover measures readily spring to mind. I will come back to these after having introduced the fourth approach of *global institutional reform*, which seems to me to hold the most promise. I will develop this approach at some length, beginning from its roots in a particular institutional understanding of human rights. The point of doing this is to clarify the moral reasons we have to be concerned about the human rights of foreigners.

An Institutional Understanding of Human Rights

A conception of human rights may be factored into two main components:

1. the *concept* of a human right used by this conception, or what one might also call its *understanding* of human rights, and
2. the *substance* or content of the conception, that is, the objects or goods it singles out for protection by a set of human rights.[6]

We face, then, two questions: What are human rights? And what human rights are there? Answers to the second question clearly presuppose an answer to the first. But the first question can, I believe, be answered without presupposing more than a vague and uncontroversial outline of an answer to the second. This, in any case, is what I attempt to do here, in order to clarify what those human rights are in the name of which the option of humanitarian intervention should be available and, if necessary, exercised.

The concept of human rights has six central features that any plausible understanding of human rights must incorporate. First, human rights express *ultimate moral* concerns: agents have a moral duty to respect human rights, a duty that does not derive from a more general moral duty to comply with national or international laws. (In fact, the opposite may hold: conformity with human rights is a moral requirement on any legal order, whose capacity to create moral obligations depends in part on such conformity.) Second, they express *weighty* moral concerns, which normally override other normative considerations. Third, these moral concerns are focused on *human beings*, as all of them and they alone have human rights and the special moral status associated therewith. Fourth, with respect to these moral concerns, all human beings have *equal status*: they have exactly the same human rights, and the moral significance of these rights and of their violations does not vary with whose human rights are at stake.[7] Fifth, human rights express moral concerns that are *unrestricted*, that is, they ought to be honored by all human agents irrespective of their particular epoch, culture, religion, moral tradition, or philosophy. Sixth, these moral concerns are *broadly sharable*, that is, capable of being understood and appreciated by persons from different epochs and cultures as well as by adherents of a variety of different religions, moral traditions, and philosophies. The notions of unrestrictedness and broad sharability are related in that we tend to feel more confident about conceiving of a moral concern as unrestricted when this concern is not parochial to some particular epoch, culture, religion, moral tradition, or philosophy.

Various understandings of human rights are consistent with these six points. The proposed institutional understanding of human rights interprets the postulate of a human right to X as the demand that every society (or comparable social system) ought to be so organized that all its participants enjoy secure access to X.[8] A human right to freedom of expression, for example, implies then that human beings have a moral claim that the institutional order of their society be maintained or reformed in such a way that they can securely exercise this freedom. To honor this claim, its citizens must ensure not merely that their government and its officials respect these freedoms, but also that limitations and violations of them on the part of other persons are effectively deterred and prevented.

On the institutional understanding I propose, your human rights are then moral claims *on* any institutional order imposed upon you and moral claims *against* those (especially more influential and privileged) persons who contribute to its imposition. You have a moral claim that any institutional order imposed upon you be so structured that you have secure access to the objects of your human rights. And you have a correlative moral responsibility that any institutional order you help impose on others be so structured that *they* have secure access to the objects of their human rights. When a society fails to realize human rights when it could, then those of its members who do not support the requisite institutional reforms are violating a negative duty of justice: the duty not to cooperate in the imposition of an unjust institutional order without making serious efforts within their means toward initiating and supporting appropriate institutional reforms or toward protecting the victims of injustice.[9]

Though somewhat unconventional, this institutional understanding of human rights accords well with the understanding implicit in the Universal Declaration of Human Rights.[10] Its article 28 reads: "Everyone is entitled to a social and international order in which the rights and freedoms set forth in this Declaration can be fully realized." As its reference to "the rights and freedoms set forth in this Declaration" indicates, this article does not add a further right to the list, but rather addresses the concept of a human right. It is then, on the one hand, consistent with any substantive account of the objects that a scheme of human rights ought to protect, but also affects, on the other hand, the meaning of any human rights postulated in the other articles. They all are to be understood as claims on the institutional order of any comprehensive social system.[11]

Though meant to be a plausible explication of Article 28, this institutional understanding of human rights is somewhat novel by being both *more* and *less* demanding than the common view according to which, by postulating a human right to X, one declares that every society ought to incorporate a right to X into its basic law or constitution and ought effectively to honor this right whether or not it is so juridified. This institutional understanding is *less* demanding by not requiring that persons enjoying secure access to X must also have a legal right thereto. Having corresponding legal rights in addition is not *so* important that this additional demand would need to be incorporated into each human right. A person's human right to adequate nutrition (Article 25), for instance, should count as fulfilled when this person has secure access to adequate nutrition, even when such access is not legally guaranteed. Insistence on juridification would not only dilute our conception of human rights through the inclusion of elements that are not truly essential, it would also provoke the communitarian and East Asian criticism that human rights lead persons to view themselves as Westerners: atomized, autonomous, secular, and self-interested individuals ready to insist on their rights no matter what the cost may be to others. Employment of the institutional understanding of human rights singles out the truly essential elements of human flourishing and, in particular, avoids any conceptual connection with legal rights. Even those hostile to a legal-rights culture can share the goal of establishing for all human beings secure access to certain vital goods.

My institutional understanding of human rights is in two respects *more* demanding than the common view. It is *more* demanding by requiring secure access even against private threats. To illustrate: even if there is an effective legal path that would allow domestic servants in India to defend themselves against abuse by their employers, many of them nevertheless cannot make use of this opportunity because they do not know what their legal rights are or lack either the knowledge or the economic independence necessary to initiate legal action. The existing institutional order fails to establish adequate social and economic safeguards, which might ensure that such servants are literate, know their rights and options, and have some economic security in case of job loss. This is a grave fault that a plausible understanding of the human right to freedom from inhuman and degrading treatment (Article 5), should be sensitive to.[12] So, according to the institutional understanding, an institutional order fails to fulfill human rights even if it merely fails sufficiently to protect their objects. By imposing an institutional order upon others, one takes responsibility for their human rights.[13]

The second, and here more relevant, respect in which this institutional understanding of human rights is *more* demanding than the common view has to do with its giving no special moral significance to national borders. This point, again, accords with Article 28. It entails that our international institutional order is to be assessed and reformed by reference to its relative contribution to human rights fulfillment.[14] Understood institutionally, human rights in our time have global normative reach — a person's human rights entail not merely moral claims on the institutional order of her own society, which are claims against her fellow *citizens*, but also analogous moral claims on the *global* institutional order, which are claims against her fellow human beings. We thus have the same kind of duties with regard to our international order as with regard to the institutional order of our own national society.

To appreciate how this last point brings out the tight association between the institutional understanding of human rights and the fourth approach to preempting humanitarian interventions, one must distinguish this point from another, more common view which also ascribes to us a responsibility for the human rights of all — demanding that we ought to defend, as best we can, the objects of the human rights of any person anywhere on earth.[15] What Article 28 is asking of the citizens and governments of the developed states is not that we assume the role of a global police force ready to intervene to aid and protect all those whose human rights are imperiled by brutal governments or civil wars, but that we support institutional reforms toward an international order that would strongly support the emergence and stability of democratic, rights-respecting, and peaceful regimes. The institutional understanding of human rights becomes international not by assessing how governments conduct their foreign policy, but by assessing how they shape international practices or institutions. It is this global institutional order that gives rise to our responsibility for the human rights of foreigners, and it is this order to which the goal of realizing human rights is most immediately assigned.

Thinking of human rights in this way makes sense only insofar as it is empirically true that the realization of human rights importantly depends on the structure of our global order and that this global order is to some extent subject to intelligent (re)design by reference to the imperative of human rights fulfillment. Returning to the examination of the fourth approach to preempting humanitarian intervention, let me then try to make plausible that these two empirical presuppositions hold, looking specifically at global institutional reforms that would reduce the occasions on which humanitarian intervention seems morally compelling.

Global Institutional Reform

Talk of a "global institutional order" sounds horribly abstract and requires at least some brief explication. There is, first and foremost, the institution of the modern state. The land surface of our planet is divided into a number of clearly demarcated and non-overlapping national territories. Human beings are matched up with these territories, so that (at least for the most part) each person belongs to exactly one territory. Any person or group effectively controlling a preponderant share of the means of coercion within a territory is recognized as the legitimate government of both the territory and the persons belonging to it. This government is entitled to rule "its" people through laws, orders, and officials; to adjudicate conflicts among them; and to exercise ultimate control over all resources within the territory ("eminent domain"). It is also entitled to represent its people against the rest of the world — to bind them *vis-à-vis* outsiders through treaties and contracts, to regulate their relations with outsiders, to declare and prosecute wars in their name, and to control outsiders' access to the country's territory. In this second role, a government is considered continuous with its predecessors and successors — bound by the undertakings of the former, and capable through its own undertakings of binding the latter. There are, of course, various minor deviations[16] and also many further, less essential features of our global order. But these most basic features will suffice for now.

This global order plays a significant role in generating the endemic under-fulfillment of human rights, which keeps the topic of humanitarian intervention on our agenda. So long as the international criterion for the legitimacy of governments is effective control, there are strong incentives to attain and to keep power by force; once in power, putschists can count on all the rewards of international recognition. They can, for example, control and hence profit from the sale of the country's natural resources. They can also borrow funds abroad in the name of the whole country and then spend these funds as they see fit. Foreign bankers need have no special worries about being repaid in the event that democracy returns, because any future government will be considered obligated to repay the loans of any predecessor and will have to comply on pains of being shut out of the international credit markets.

Could we modify our global order so that it contributes better to the stability of democratic governments? One might begin by incorporating into international law the option for countries to declare that they assume no responsibility for repaying loans incurred by a future government that will have ruled in violation of constitutionally prescribed democratic procedures. This principle prevents neither putschists from coming to power nor lenders from loaning money to putschists. But it does render such loans considerably more risky and thereby entails that putschists can borrow less—and this on less favorable terms. It thus reduces the staying power of undemocratic governments and the incentives for attempting a coup in the first place.

It may be said that this idea could be just as well implemented pursuant to the third approach—through *local* rather than global institutional reform. The current democratic government of Brazil, say, could unilaterally make such a declaration and could even seek to amend Brazil's constitution so as to make it unconstitutional for any future Brazilian government to repay loans incurred by undemocratic or unconstitutional predecessor regimes.

In response, unilateral strategies of this sort are indeed viable and, I think, should be explored and employed far more than they are today. Still, global institutional reform, though harder to pull off, has three important advantages. First, it provides assurance. By specifically recognizing the right of a democratically elected government to make such a declaration, all governments undertake not to put pressure on future democratic governments to repay the loans of illegitimate predecessors. This strengthens the incentive against lending money to illegitimate regimes and hence also the incentive against seeking to grab power by force.

Second, the global approach could, and should, include the instituting of a neutral council that would determine, in an internationally authoritative way, whether a particular government is constitutional or not.[17] This council might be fashioned on the model of the International Court of Justice in The Hague, but it should also have specially trained personnel for observing—and in special cases even conducting—national elections. Democratic governments could facilitate the work of the council, and thereby contribute to the stability of democracy in their country, by incorporating into their written constitutions clear legitimacy criteria that also fix precisely how these criteria can be legitimately revised.

Thirdly, the global approach can also help remove a disadvantage of the contemplated reform through which it is liable to have a destabilizing influence on existing democratic governments. Such an influence might come about as follows. If an officially illegitimate government cannot, in any case, borrow abroad in the name of the entire country, it may see no reason to service debts incurred by its democratic predecessors. Anticipating this fact, foreign lenders may then be reluctant to give loans to democratic governments perceived to be in danger of being overthrown—which would not be, of course, in the spirit of my proposal.[18] This difficulty might be neutralized through an international loan insurance fund that services the debts of democratically legitimate governments whenever illegitimate successors refuse to do so. The fund, just as the council proposed above, should be financed jointly by all democratic states. This would require some states, the enduringly stable democracies, to contribute to a fund from which they will hardly ever profit directly. Their financial contribution would, however, be small, because my proposal would render the overthrow of democratic regimes much less frequent. And their financial contribution would also be well justified in view of the gain for democratization, which would bring with it gains for the fulfillment of human rights and the avoidance of wars and civil wars, whereby it would also reduce the incidence of occasions for—often costly—humanitarian interventions.

It is more difficult to design a reform that would enable democratic governments to prevent illegitimate successors from selling the country's natural resources. In this regard a local reform pursuant to the third approach seems entirely impossible. The only thing that could work is an international agreement not to recognize property rights in natural resources that were purchased from undemocratic and unconstitutional governments (e.g., crude oil bought from Sani Abacha). The difficulty is to enforce such an agreement especially in the case of resources whose origin cannot easily be ascertained.

Even if such global reforms succeed, Farer and Hoffmann's idea of pre-authorized military interventions might still be useful, but it should be employed somewhat differently from what they envision, in two respects. First, the decision about whether an intervention is called for, and presumably also the intervention itself, should be made by an international council (of the sort described before) rather than by a particular government whose decisions are bound to be influenced by partisan considerations. This modification would make the pre-authorization option more palatable to many countries and would also increase the deterrent effect of pre-authorizations by blocking the hope to avoid intervention through concessions unrelated to human-rights fulfillment. Second, pre-authorized interventions should function in combination with the other anti-takeover measures. This maximizes the deterrent effect of the proposal overall. And it offers the hope that, should deterrence fail, the illegitimate rulers can be brought down by the economic measures alone, *before* a pre-authorized intervention need be undertaken as a last resort. The consequent reduction in the incidence of pre-authorized interventions (relative to the Farer/Hoffmann proposal) is a further gain, because military interventions will, sometimes at least, themselves be costly in human-rights terms.

Conclusion

The moral question generally asked about humanitarian intervention is: under what conditions, to what extent, and in what form is humanitarian intervention morally permissible? This question tends to lead to arguments between those who hold that an adequate international ethic should impose somewhat weaker constraints upon humanitarian interventions than current international law and those who hold that, since military interventions will in many cases produce more harm than good and will set dangerous precedents, there sadly is little we can do about the deplorable global state of human-rights fulfillment.[19] If we truly care about the fulfillment of human rights, we must go beyond this question and think also about reforms of our global institutional order, which can greatly reduce the occasions for humanitarian intervention by providing strong incentives to national societies toward fulfilling the human rights of their members. In this regard, the wealthy democracies have a duty to intervene at the level of global institutional design. Insofar as they ignore this duty by continuing to support the existing international order, they share responsibility for the underfulfillment of human rights it engenders.

Notes

1. Felix Oppenheim has done much to develop an account of the national interest that satisfies these two conditions, i.e., that it is acceptable to citizens and politicians across much of the political spectrum and also clear and specific enough to facilitate consensus on how foreign-policy outcomes should be assessed by reference to it. (Oppenheim accepts that *ex ante* assessments of foreign-policy options by reference to the national interest so defined must remain controversial because of the other two complexities, of facts and of means.) Having had many engaging and highly productive written and oral exchanges on this issue with Professor Oppenheim over many years, I am still not convinced that his project can succeed. Irrespective of this disagreement, my claim in the text is true so long as Oppenheim's project has not in fact succeeded—specifically, so long as his conception of the national interest has not come to be widely accepted. If his project were to succeed, the second complexity of diplomacy would indeed have been overcome. Cf. Felix Oppenheim, *The Place of Morality in Foreign Policy* (Lexington, KY: Lexington Books 1991) 10-15, as well as his forthcoming essay "The National Interest: A Basic Concept." Oppenheim's project is further discussed in George Kateb's contribution to the present volume.

2. This is a general point. Having a known disposition to promote a certain goal may get in the way of the promotion of this goal. Thus, your overwhelmingly powerful motive to protect your daughter may make her a preferred kidnapping target.

3. One such rare instance was the public debate over China's most-favored nation status, during which some of the strategic aspects of the relationship were attended to in the media. We may recall here the old joke about the inmates of a zoo or asylum who view their own conduct as successfully conditioning the behavior of the wardens, just as the wardens view themselves as successfully manipulating the behavior of the inmates.

4. For a brief discussion, see Derek Parfit, *Reasons and Persons* (Oxford: Oxford University Press 1984) section 8.

5. Tom J. Farer, "The United States as Guarantor of Democracy in the Caribbean Basin: Is There a Legal Way?," *Human Rights Quarterly* 10.12 (1988): 157-76; Tom J. Farer, "A Paradigm of Legitimate Intervention," *Enforcing Restraint: Collective Intervention in Internal Conflicts*, ed. Lori Fisler Damrosch (New York: Council on Foreign Relations Press 1993) 316-47; Stanley Hoffmann, "Delusions of World Order," *New York Review of Books* 39.7 (1992) 37-43; and Stanley Hoffmann, *The Ethics and Politics of Humanitarian Intervention* (Notre Dame, IN: University of Notre Dame Press 1996).

6. Here the *object* of a human right is whatever this human right is a right to — adequate nutrition, for example, or physical integrity.

7. This second component of equality is compatible with the view that the weight agents ought to give to the human rights of others varies with their relation to them — that agents have stronger moral reasons to secure human rights in their own country, for example, than abroad — so long as this is not seen as being due to a difference in the moral significance of these rights, impersonally considered. (One can consistently believe that the flourishing of all children is equally important and also that one should show special concern for the flourishing of one's own children.)

8. What matters is secure access to the objects of human rights, rather than these objects themselves, because an institutional order is not morally problematic merely because some of its participants are choosing to fast or to compete in boxing matches. Moreover, no society can make the objects of all human rights absolutely secure. And making them as secure as possible would constitute a ludicrous drain on societal resources for what, at the margins, would be very minor benefits in security. To be plausible, any conception of human rights that uses the concept I propose must therefore incorporate an idea of reasonable security thresholds. Your human rights are fulfilled when their objects are sufficiently secure — with the required degrees of security suitably adapted to the means and circumstances of the relevant social system. Thus, your human right to freedom of peaceful assembly and association is fulfilled, when it is sufficiently unlikely that your attempts to associate or assemble with others would be thwarted or punished by official or nonofficial agents or agencies. The task of making this idea more precise for each particular human right belongs to the second, substantive component of a conception of human rights.

9. The institutional understanding of human rights sketched in the last four paragraphs is more extensively elaborated in my "How Should Human Rights be Conceived?," *Jahrbuch für Recht und Ethik* 3 (1995): 103-20.

10. Adopted and proclaimed by the General Assembly of the United Nations on December 10, 1948, as resolution 217A(III).

11. One can get from Article 28 to my institutional understanding of human rights by making four plausible interpretive conjectures. (1) Alternative institutional orders that do not satisfy the requirement of Article 28 can be ranked by how close they come to fully realizing human rights; social systems ought to be structured so that human rights can be realized in them as fully as possible. (2) How fully human rights can be realized in some institutional order is measured by how fully these human rights generally are, or (in the case of a hypothetical

institutional order) generally would be, realized in it. (3) An institutional order realizes a human right insofar as (and fully if and only if) this human right is fulfilled for the persons upon whom this order is imposed. (4) A human right is fulfilled for some person if and only if this person enjoys secure access to its object. Taking these four conjectures together, we see that human rights can be fully realized in some institutional order if and only if this order affords all those upon whom it is imposed secure access to the objects of their human rights.

12. Similarly, and closer to home, a plausible understanding of human rights should also be sensitive to an institutional order that does not adequately prevent and deter domestic violence.

13. And yet, an institutional order is nevertheless more unjust when it officially authorizes or even mandates avoidably insecure access to the objects of human rights than when it allows the same insecurity to result from insufficient prevention or deterrence. This differential weighing is deeply rooted in our moral thinking and shows itself, for instance, in our attitudes toward the criminal law and the penal system. Harms done to innocents which are inflicted in the course of police work or through official punishments weigh more heavily than equal harms inflicted on them through "private" crimes not sufficiently prevented and deterred by the penal system. Our institutional order and its political and legal organs should not merely serve justice, but also symbolize it. This point is important, because it undermines the plausibility of consequentialist and hypothetical-contract (e.g., Rawls) conceptions of justice which assess an institutional order from the standpoint of prudent prospective participants, who, of course, have no reason to care about this distinction among sources of insecurity. Cf. Thomas W. Pogge, "Three Problems with Contractarian-Consequentialist Ways of Assessing Social Institutions," *Social Philosophy and Policy* 12.2 (1995): 241-66, esp. section 5. We must avoid the mistake of many consequentialist and contractualist conceptions of justice which base the moral assessment of an institutional order solely on the magnitude of the benefits and burdens it "distributes" to persons while ignoring the nature of the relation between that order and these pay-offs. A plausible conception of human rights must then establish not only a scheme of vital goods (to be recognized as objects of human rights), but also a method for weighting shortfalls from secure access which takes account of the different kinds of connections between institutional schemes and human-rights fulfillment.

14. "Relative," because what matters is how well an institutional scheme does in comparison to its feasible alternatives.

15. The concept of human rights is so understood, for example, by Luban: "A human right, then, will be a right whose beneficiaries are all humans and whose obligors are all humans in a position to effect the right"; David Luban, "Just War and Human Rights," *International Ethics*, ed. Charles Beitz et al. (Princeton, NJ: Princeton University Press 1985) 195-216, at 209. This view is more radical than mine, because it does not make the global normative reach of human rights conditional upon the existence of a worldwide institutional order in whose coercive imposition we collaborate.

16. There are stateless persons, persons with multiple nationalities, and those who are citizens of one country but reside in or are visiting another. We have Antarctica, continental shelves, disputed areas, and areas that are contracted out (such as Guantanamo Bay and Hong Kong, though the latter case is also a beautiful illustration of the continuity condition). And groups are sometimes recognized as the legitimate government even though they do not control a preponderant share of the means of coercion within the relevant territory (Pol Pot's Khmer Rouge in the 1980s or Bertrand Aristide in the 1990s).

17. This council would, of course, work only in the interest of democratic constitutions. Its determinations would have consequences not only for a government's ability to borrow

abroad, but also for its domestic and international standing. A government that has been officially declared illegitimate would be handicapped in myriad ways (trade, diplomacy, investments, etc.) — a fact that would contribute to the deterrent effect of the proposed institutional innovation and hence to its tendency to reduce the risk of coup attempts.

18. Thanks are due to Ronald Dworkin for seeing this difficulty and for articulating it forcefully.

19. See, for example, the exchange between Michael Walzer — defending the latter view in *Just and Unjust Wars* (New York: Basic Books 1977), and in "The Moral Standing of States," *Philosophy and Public Affairs* 9 (1980): 209-29 — and the critics he responds to in the latter piece: Charles Beitz, Gerald Doppelt, David Luban, and Richard Wasserstrom. See also the meta-responses by two of the criticized critics — David Luban, "The Romance of the Nation State," *Philosophy and Public Affairs* 9 (1980): 392-97; and Charles Beitz, "Cosmopolitan Ideals and National Sentiment," *Journal of Philosophy* 80 (1983): 591-600.

6

Humanitarian Intervention and International Law

Alfred P. Rubin

There are so many problems with analyzing when and where "humanitarian intervention" might be "justified" as a matter of public international law that is it very difficult to know where to begin. "Justified" is itself a word in the moral order as well as in the legal order. What may be "justified" morally might be illegal, and what is "justified" legally might still be immoral. But notions of the "international legal order" in the minds of many include what others regard as "moral" rules, which they differentiate from "legal" rules.

To understand what is "justified" in international affairs law, it is necessary first to ask how the international legal order works and how the international moral order works and whether we, individually, see a distinction between the two. If we do, then Occam's Razor[1] forces us to seek the simplest explanation or theory. Let us begin, then, by asking, "What is public international law?"

To a "positivist" jurist, public international law is fundamentally those "rules" agreed by humans to be the rules that they undertake to obey in their activities as statespeople. Of course, the notion that "agreement" to rules makes those rules "binding" in any normative order, is itself a "rule" of rule-formation, and rests on assumptions and convenience; so "positive law" is inherently based on "natural law" assumptions. Thus, even assuming that otherwise "positive" law is the simplest model for the international legal order, and ignoring the weakness of its roots as a complete system, there is a level of rules beyond that, rules that exist in the practical world of affairs regardless of the will of jurists, rules of "natural law." To many statespeople and jurists, those are rules of the individual or collective conscience, rules in the moral order, which cannot be changed by treaties or other evidence of the agreement of statespeople: *jus cogens*. The major problem with this latter, "natural law," approach (one problem of many) is that rules of conscience vary with the consciences of those asserting the "rules" to be binding on themselves or others.

But it is common experience that consciences do in fact vary. Moral rules seem to reflect value systems, and choosing among competing values affected by a particular course of action leads us into areas of grave dispute among learned and honorable people.[2] Moreover, a more "honorable" course depends on whether those who see a benefit to themselves and do not share in others' perceptions of honor or virtue will benefit; the ultimate result might well be dishonor to those whose notion of "honor" is most keen.[3] Even that conclusion rests on an analysis of *whose* conception of "honor" is to be the measure of virtue, and depends also on what values are involved in that determination of what "honor" is.

And yet, it is frequently asserted that there are some acts so heinous (Nazi racism coupled with Nazi extermination policies applied to those, like Jews and gypsies, who were defined as members of "inferior races") that "humanitarian intervention" to rescue the endangered "inferiors" is morally, and perhaps even legally, justified. The issue to both "naturalist" and "positivist" international lawyers, as always, is who determines that the need for such intervention is indeed "humanitarian," that the perception of values by those against whom the intervention is aimed is so perverted that it is morally or legally justifiable to kill or otherwise disempower them, that the death of our own children and the expenditure of our own money is a lesser value than the good being done by killing others.

Indeed, there is yet another factor to be considered: whether all the "enemy" or their friends are proper targets for the intervention. For example, was it morally justifiable to drop a nuclear weapon on Japan at the end of World War II, killing many children and other non-combatants who were nonetheless part of the "community" of the evil doers, in order to save "our" lives even in what was regarded by the people ordering the bomb to be dropped as a just war of self-defense.[4]

Yet another "natural law" approach is the "divine law" approach. Some statespeople are so convinced that they are privy to the will of a superior impersonal lawgiver, whom they and others might call "God" or "history" or "economics," that killing others or destroying property to help achieve that lawgiver's special pattern or plan is regarded as "humanitarian" in the long run. By this logic, the killer behaves morally; pain and suffering of others, or even of the killer him/herself, is rationalized as unavoidable in the long run, and present killing or destruction of property is regarded by the actor(s) as morally the lesser evil than awaiting the assured death and destruction that he or she believes is certain to come in fulfillment of the divine, historical, economic, or other "objectively" perceived plan.

Yet another "natural law" approach is that by which the "law of gravity" or the "laws of human nature" are equated with divine law. By this approach, human ambition and ruthlessness among many other things are regarded as inevitable, and the only issue remaining is to determine whose will is to dominate. By this approach, the "struggle" for authority and dominance is "wired" into us, and any attempt to short-circuit the wiring will surely fail; successful short-circuitry will bring to the top of an authority structure those unable to discharge its "natural law" obligations and lead to uncertainty, instability, and general misery.

I have serious problems with the entire "natural law" approach to group behavior. As a moralist, I must regard my own conscience as my own guide, but not a guide for others, who have their own consciences. Basic to this approach is a firm belief in my own fallibility, odd as that might seem. The logic is as follows:

I know that I am fallible; I am a younger brother, and my big brother made my fallibility clear to me before I was three years old. I thought he was infallible when he was five or six. But by the time I was five or six, I had realized my big brother's fallibility. At that point, I accepted the infallibility of my parents. That infallibility disappeared when I was 13 or 14 years old. But my own sense of fallibility has remained.

From that fallibility flow two inferences:

1. If I am fallible, my brother is fallible, and my parents were fallible, I can infer that it is likely (not certain, but certainly likely) that others are fallible, too. That includes religious leaders as well as secular leaders. It means that majority rule is a rule of convenience, not a rule of infallibility. The effect of a majority decision, then, is defined by the system in which that decision is made; it might be determinative of fact or law within the system, but might not. And it is certainly irrelevant to my own moral rules and to whatever rules of true natural law might exist. A majority might purport to repeal the "law of gravity," but if I step out of an airplane, I fall down regardless of the view of a majority as to the law of gravity. The law of gravity operates in the natural order, not the moral or positive or in the religiously defined divine law order (at least, as far as can be demonstrated today). Similarly, the "laws of economics" or of history operate regardless of human activity; they certainly take account of human activity, but we cannot change the "laws," if they exist.

2. From all this it follows that even when confronted with an airtight, infallible argument, I must be satisfied myself as to its value in whatever order I perceive as applicable. The reason is not that the person presenting the argument is necessarily fallible—she or he might not be fallible. The reason is that I cannot know the truth because I am fallible. So, if I am convinced that somebody else is right about Jews or Palestinians, I might still be wrong. That is not to

say that the other person is necessarily wrong, but that I cannot know that he or she is right because even if I am convinced of his/her rightness, I might be wrong about that because I am, after all, fallible.

The "natural law" notions of humanitarian intervention thus seem to rest on the assumption that some acts are perceived by all human beings as so horrible that they must be forbidden by a universal natural law. Let us take "murder" as an example.

Even "murder" admits of a large area of doubt that perhaps covers the entire concept. Is it "murder" to kill in self-defense? What about defense of the immediate family — at least helpless children in that family? What about defense of the helpless stranger in a wheelchair? The person who might not seem helpless, but seems certain to be killed by another anyhow? And what is "family"? Can I defend a close friend about to be killed? A member of my tribe? My country? Is a "murder" committed by any person who believes in the moral justifiability of his/her acts? Are soldiers ever committing "murder" if they kill to preserve what they believe to be their country? "*Dolce et decorum est, pro patria mori*," as Horace once wrote, to widespread approval not only in Roman times, but in modern times as well.[5] In a sense, the play cited in note 4 above, *Copenhagen* by Michael Frayn, is based on this objection.

There is yet another problem: whose determination counts when trying to see if a particular "murder" has been justifiable? If "justifiable" is meant in the moral order, then the determination of the murderer him/herself would seem to be the determinative factor. The "murderer" will be condemned by those who disagree, but to him/herself will appear to be all right. He or she will have a clear conscience. If "justifiable" reflects the view of a community, then the moral penalties of opprobrium and perhaps isolation will be felt by the killer, whatever the state of his/her conscience. If "justifiable" is conceived as a word in the positive legal order, then the positive legal remedies will apply and the decision will be made by a judge, jury, or whoever the legal order entrusts with that judgment.

There are at least two objects to be achieved by our legal order: the well-being and cohesion of the law-making/law-interpreting/law-enforcing community on the one hand, and the well-being of individual members of that community. Of course, in some communities, like that in the US, the well-being of individuals is considered to be an aspect of the well-being of the community as a whole, but its legal system nonetheless is divided into two aspects: criminal and civil. To keep the community in order, incorrigibles might be imprisoned, or those capable of reforming are sought to be reformed, or otherwise anti-community behavior is deterred by punishment or the threat of various sorts of punishment. To keep individual or corporate members of the community content, there is a parallel system of civil remedies, which depend initially on the willingness (in some cases apparently the desire) of the self-identified "victim" to take money payment as compensation for the evil he, she, or they think was done by a malefactor. Civil cases are brought or not brought as the supposed victim chooses, not as the state or other collectivity decides. Criminal actions are brought by the state normally regardless of the will of the supposed victim (and some "crimes" against the community are otherwise "victimless"). We have all seen an example of that when O.J. Simpson was acquitted of criminal charges by means of the positive law, yet was convicted by the press and a civil jury in a case brought by the nearest relatives of those he was found by the civil jury to have killed.

If these complexities cannot be resolved to universal satisfaction in a legal order wholly controlled by Americans, then it is vain to expect a resolution to be acceptable to all in the international legal order, which is not wholly controlled by any single party or group.

Taking this approach, thus, there does not seem to be any universal prohibition of "murder." And if the asserted universal prohibition on "murder" is not clear, then are any other of the prohibitions in the Judeo-Christian-Muslim 10 Commandments any clearer? Is there universal agreement as to the meaning of operative terms? Is there universal agreement as to whose determination of the meaning of those terms is to be applied to others, other than the person making the determination and those bound by the positive law to accept that determination? Those who think in terms of the "international community" would do well to recall that about one-fifth of the world community is Chinese, another fifth or so Hindu Indian, and yet another fifth various radical religious groups whose notion of morality rests on the interpretation of some holy writ, be it the Jewish Bible, the New Testament, the Quran, or anything similar to any particular group. Yet three-fifths is a majority, and to those who would argue that many Chinese or Indians reject the teachings of their selected or elected leaders, the obvious response is that so do many American and Europeans reject the teachings of theirs.

All of this is preliminary to questions of humanitarian intervention as a matter of positive law in the international arena.

The United Nations Charter is a treaty, formally "accepted as law" by nearly all states in the world.[6] Now, let us assume that that express or implied "agreement" is a "law-making" process by which those agreeing are bound by their own word to accept a particular rule as "binding." As noted above, however illogical or "natural law" or "moral law" based, that is the fundamental assumption of the positive law.

The UN Charter has in it both substantive terms and a constitution-like delegation of authority, just as the American Constitution has substantive terms and terms that delegate law-making authority to the Congress, and law-interpreting and enforcing authority to the executive and judicial branches of the American government.

Under the agreed distribution of authority in the UN Charter, the Security Council can authorize the use of force. But whether that authority extends to cases of humanitarian intervention can be a matter of considerable doubt to a true "positivist" international lawyer.

Under article 24 of the Charter, the states members of the UN have agreed that the Security Council has "primary responsibility for the maintenance of international peace and security."[7] Under article 25, members agreed "to accept and carry out the decisions of the Security Council in accordance with the present Charter." Leaving aside the positivist question as to whether the phrase "in accordance with the present Charter" modifies "carry out" or "decisions" or both, in one highly emotional and politically involved case, the International Court of Justice held very narrowly that a "decision" could be made by the Security Council even without using the word "decision."[8]

The use of force by the "decision" of the Security Council seems even more narrowly proscribed. Article 41 of the Charter allows the Security Council to "decide what measures not involving the use of armed force are to be employed to give effect to its decisions." Assuming that all concerned agree (at least implicitly, by silence) that the Security Council has made a "decision," article 42 allows the Security Council to "take such action by air, sea, or land forces as may be necessary to maintain or restore international peace and security" when it considers that measures provided for in article 41 would be (or have proved to be) inadequate. Presumably the inadequacy refers to giving effect to its prior "decision" on any subject, although, reading article 42 carefully, it might relate to a "decision" involving international peace and security only.

"Decisions" of the Security Council in substantive matters are made by the vote of the Council. Of the 15 members, five are "permanent," reflecting the views of the victors of World War II in 1945: the Republic of China (since replaced by the People's Republic of China), France, the United Kingdom, the US, and the Union of Soviet Socialist Republics (since replaced by Russia). All five must vote in favor of the measures or abstain[9] for a "decision" (under any definition) to be adopted by the Security Council. The views of advocates as to the "humanitarian" aspects of a situation are irrelevant under the Charter; only the votes of members of the Security Council count. Of course, those votes can be influenced by lobbying pressures from convinced humanitarians, but they can also be influenced by lobbying pressures from others and by calculations of inhumane politics and sheer miscalculations or disagreements as to the humanitarian content of any particular situation. For example, is assistance to a police force "humanitarian" if the job of the police under its municipal law authority is not only to inhibit the murder of innocent bystanders, but also to help maintain an existing power structure that considers the wealth of the leaders of that structure to be a higher value to its society than the well-being of the society's workers and their families? Or only those of the workers and their families that can trace their descent from a particular tribe or group of ancestors? Is "apartheid," or racial discrimination, to be regarded as forbidden by international law? Why? The moral condemnation repeated often enough by the UN General Assembly is not positive law under the terms of the UN Charter. Indeed, it is doubtful that many states would have voted to condemn such discrimination if they had thought the condemnation would apply to themselves. Yet many states practice such discrimination, including many of those most loudly condemning it. This is not to say that racial discrimination (even if it were possible to define "race" or "discrimination" to universal satisfaction, which it probably is not) is morally acceptable behavior. It is up to each unit in the system to decide for itself what is morally acceptable to it, which is to say that there are serious doubts as to whether such discrimination violates "international law."

There are some "human rights" documents that have become part of the "positive law" by agreement in the form needed within the international legal order to enact positive law. Some frequently cited are not legally binding at all.[10] Others are binding on the parties and have proved effective in some ways, normally if accompanied by some enforcement mechanism that uses the discretion of others than the accused or the accuser(s) to determine the meaning of the agreement and whether the facts in any particular situation implicate it.[11] Still other treaties are widely ratified, but contain terms that restrict their utility to far less than the "human rights" advocates would like.[12] For example, in the Genocide Convention, it is not the international community that can intervene in a genocidal event; under Article VII of the Convention: "Persons charged with genocide ... shall be tried by a competent tribunal of the State in the territory of which the act was committed, or by such international penal tribunal as may have jurisdiction with respect to those Contracting Parties which shall have accepted its jurisdiction." Obviously, it is the states parties that control enforcement; "jurisdiction to adjudicate" is restricted by the very terms of the defining document itself to the states directly involved. The reference to an international penal tribunal is restricted to cases in which the states involved have agreed by positive law to accepting the jurisdiction of such a tribunal. Similarly, in the Convention forbidding racial discrimination, it is left to the states parties themselves to "take effective measures to review governmental ... policies, and to amend ... any laws which have the effect of creating or perpetuating racial discrimination"[13] Many other undertakings are the responsibilities of the states parties, but no party seems to have the requisite "standing" to question the performance of any other party, and a "Committee on the Elimination of Racial Discrimination" is established with the authority merely to consider complaints—and even that authority depends on a state party declaring that it "recognizes the competence of the Committee to receive and consider communications from individuals or groups of individuals within its jurisdiction claiming to be victims of a violation by that State Party ... No communication shall be received by the Committee if it concerns a State Party which has not made such a declaration."[14]

It would seem that the most effective tools for handling "humanitarian" issues accept the notion of continuing state responsibility and adapt to it. Thus the Final Act of the Conference on Security and Co-Operation in Europe (Helsinki Accords) of 1 August 1975[15] does not purport to be a treaty, binding states to substantive terms as a matter of positive law, but provides instead for further conferences on the subjects covered by the Act, at which the agenda can be adjusted by any party in order to have the group examine the progress made by other states parties toward achieving the goals agreed in general terms in the Convention. The goals are to be met individually by states, and there is no tribunal involved. The issue is apparently solved by the inadvertence of the parties involved overcoming the hurdle of "standing." The hurdle was in fact overcome by allowing parties to inscribe the progress of others in the agenda without actually pressing any claims or purporting to represent any supposed "victims" in their claims against their own government.

Similarly, in the four positive law-of-war conventions concluded in Geneva in 1949,[16] provision is made in identical language for states parties to search for persons alleged to have committed or ordered to be committed various "grave breaches" (listed atrocities) and to "bring such persons, regardless of their nationality, before its own courts." No provision is made for producing evidence either to support the allegations or to serve as defenses against the allegations, and no such case has been brought in a third-country's court in the 50 years the conventions have been in force. Alternatively, a party may, "if it prefers, and in accordance with the provisions of its own legislation, hand such persons over for trial to another High Contracting Party concerned, provided such High Contracting Party has made out a *prima facie* case."[17] Again, no such case is known ever to have occurred. Indeed, the quoted language seems designed to be obscure, if not meaningless. Can a state be obliged to try an alleged perpetrator without having made out a *prima facie* case itself? The distinction between the provision for each party to search out an alleged grave breacher and bring him/her before its courts, and the discretion to hand him/her over only to another state "concerned" who has made out a *prima facie* case, seems to imply a major distinction. How can a state be obliged to try an alleged grave breacher without itself establishing a *prima facie* case at least to its own satisfaction? Who is a "Party concerned" — is that a disguised reference to "standing"? Who judges whether a *"prima facie* case" has in fact been made out? And these are only a few of the many questions that could be raised in trying to interpret this language or translate it into provisions that would operate in the real world. It is simply not persuasive to cite or repeat the interpretations of those who place their conceptions of "human rights" above the customary law division of the world into "states" or municipal legal orders, each with its own criminal law system and its own civil law system.

The UN Security Council has played many games with the wording of the UN Charter and radically expanded its authority by its own interpretations of it. For example, today the Security Council seems almost routinely to recite that it is acting under its authority contained in Chapter VII of the Charter. But that authority goes only to issues involving threats to the peace, breaches of the peace, or acts of aggression. Some actions of the Security Council seem only remotely, if at all, connected with world peace and security.[18]

From all this, and much more than can be compressed into an article, I would argue that the attempt to place the UN Security Council in a position of upholding "humanitarian" concerns is bound to fail as past attempts have failed. The judgment of the voting members of the Security Council is not based solely on humanitarian considerations. It must take account also of political and legal considerations. If it does not, the members of the Security Council might fancy themselves rulers of the universe, but all of them have successful revolutions in their histories and would be tempted to deny the same opportunity to others. If "democracy" is a value supported by humanitarians, then the death and destruction that goes with revolution must be permitted also, horrible as it may be, especially to the established elite and its foreign friends.

There are alternatives that might work better, as the Helsinki Accords, not even a treaty, helped to end human rights abuses in Eastern Europe. Briefly, legal defaults seem to require legal remedies. Legal remedies might exist in the civil (damages) side, if the moralists among us were prepared to allow a prospective "plaintiff " to abandon his/her case. They might exist also if the moralists among us were prepared to accept the implications of the existence of a "world community" consensus and the need for cohesion that would support "criminal" remedies. So far, all the evidence and historical likelihood shout against that notion of a world community. Are the moralists among us willing to accept a loss of control over their own moral convictions and the possibility, even likelihood, that a "populist" majority would approve of some slaughters or rigidities? Or do they believe that they are infallible, that their insights into moral values are so reasonable that they must be shared by all people? A majority of people? Does that majority include religious groups who firmly believe in their own interpretations of God's word? Even if their God has abandoned the Hutus, the Jews, the Muslims in India? Dissenting Muslims in Afghanistan? Catholics (one must not forget the 30 Years War in Europe or events in Northern Ireland today)?

I would suggest that the international legal order's "legal" remedies for human rights violations are no remedies at all, but that the remedies made available by municipal legal orders and the remedies made available by the "moral order" have worked remarkably well when used. Those remedies involve things like exposure — Helsinki-like conferences that avoid the ancient legal requirement for "standing" in civil cases or shared community values, legislators, definitive interpreters, or enforcers of the "law" for the international equivalent of a criminal action; or national or even international truth and reconciliation commissions, perhaps; or individual or national boycotts or restrictive regulations, like the Sullivan Rules that the US imposed in its municipal law on American firms wanting to do business with apartheid-laden South Africa;[19] or CoCom-like agreements of like-thinking states to restrict competitors leaping in to snaffle contracts that are unpalatable to their friends for moral reasons,[20] even if those reasons are not fully shared by the friends. Individual "grave breachers" can be denied visas; it is frequently forgotten that Kurt Waldheim was never convicted of anything by anybody, but cannot leave his own lovely country to collect the ceremonial dinners and gold watches that his career as twice-elected Secretary-General of the United Nations and President of Austria might have led him to think he would ultimately collect. Idi Amin is living out his miserable life in Saudi Arabia, last I heard, but his return to Uganda is not within the future plans of his supporters, and human remedies seem inadequate to his behavior.

Does this mean that there are some acts which we may regard as unpardonable atrocities for which there is no remedy in international law, no "right to intervene" in the internal affairs of a state bent on genocide? Probably. But that need not dissuade us from opening our doors to refugees and using what tools our municipal legal orders and the international moral and political orders give us to attempt to ameliorate those situations in which we cannot legally intervene. At least, we can remember and explain to those who have had the advantage of the horrors committed by their parents why it is that we will not deal with them.

It does not diminish our horror to know that some horrors are beyond our control. But in fact some are. Nor can the historical record ever be fully balanced. As US President Thomas Jefferson once wrote: "I tremble for my country when I reflect that God is just."[21] We all have profited from the villainies of some of our ancestors — after all, we are the descendants of those who survived, and survival frequently involved a race to the oasis with the loser dying, or a monopoly of the corn supply in times of shortage. It is well to remember that the eternal scales of justice are never balanced to universal satisfaction, and, in my opinion, the potential evils of allowing "humanitarian intervention" at the behest of any political body or decision-maker is much more likely to increase misery than to alleviate it. The only "cure" for horrors like those that occurred in Rwanda, or even in the former Yugoslavia, is not third-party intervention without standing, but deterrence by exposure and embarrassment. That is not a solution, but it is better than having one's own children dying in a struggle they do not understand, and becoming the despised "colonial" masters of a people bent on mutual destruction.

Notes

1. "*Essentia non sunt multiplicanda praeter necessitatem.*" William of Occam was an English cleric who died in 1349. Occam's Razor is formulated in terms of neo-Platonic "essences" but today is usually taken to mean that, of various possible theoretical explanations of natural or intellectual phenomena, the simplest explanation with fewest exceptions is the one we should assume to be valid, and then we should not hesitate to switch to a simpler rule if exceptions seem to weigh down the one we have been assuming.

2. See Alfred P. Rubin, "Enforcing the Rules of International Law," *Harvard International Law Journal* 34.1 (Winter 1993): 149-62, esp. 152-53; Alfred P. Rubin, *Ethics and Authority in International Law* (Cambridge: Cambridge University Press, 1997) *passim*.

3. The evils of "imperialism," the notion that rules can or should be made reflecting constituents' consciences in London or Paris to determine action by others who do not share in the hierarchy of values (whether European or not) in Africa or India, are too well-known today to require analysis. Those interested in this notion might note the self-assurance of Captain Sherard Osborne, a British naval officer, publishing in 1857 about his role in events in the Malay Peninsula in the 1830s:

> Such are the cruelties perpetrated by these wretched native monarchies … and yet philanthropists and politicians at home maunder about the unjust invasion of native rights, and preach against the extension of our rule. As if our Government, in its most corrupt form, would not be a blessing in such a region, and as much if not more, our duty to extend, as a Christian people, than to allow them to remain under native rules, and then to shoot them for following native habits.

See, Sherard Osborne, *The Blockade of Quedah*, 2nd ed. (London, 1857, 1860) 193.

4. This is the moral problem examined movingly in Michael Frayn's play, *Copenhagen*, in which an ethnic German disciple of a part-Jewish physicist in Denmark agonizes over whether his duty as a German includes a duty to obey the leadership he despises in his country. It is a true story and reflects different views and recollections of Werner von Heisenberg and Niels Bohr. The American bombs dropped on Hiroshima and Nagasaki are mentioned.

5. "It is sweet and fitting to die for one's country"—Horace, *Odes*, III.ii.13 ("Dulce et decorum est pro patria mori"); objections to Horace's approach appeared not only in England during World War I but in Germany under Hitler's regime. See Wilfred Owen, *The Collected Poems of Wilfred Owen* (New York: New Directions, 1963) 55 (mocking the quotation from

Horace in light of Owen's personal experience of the horrors of World War I; Owen was killed on 4 November 1918).

6. There are some states, universally (or nearly so) "recognized" as such, which have not agreed to the distribution of authority contained in the UN Charter. The prime example for many years has been, of course, Switzerland. Liechtenstein has been party to a case before the International Court of Justice, whose jurisdiction in such cases extends only to states. The Nottebohm Case, *Liechtenstein v. Guatemala* [1955] ICJ Reports 5. Nothing prevents the Court from accepting the petition of other non-members of the UN as "states."

7. Under the "Uniting for Peace" Resolution of 1950, the General Assembly of the UN, a body composed of all the members of the organization, asserted that when the Security Council cannot discharge that "primary responsibility" because of a veto by a permanent member (see below), responsibility for the maintenance of international peace and security passes to the General Assembly. Whether that self-promoting resolution makes entire logical sense is no longer a serious issue; the General Assembly successfully utilized that authority throughout the Korean War after it was passed, and it hardly seems questioned today. See Leo Gross, "Voting in the Security Council: Abstention from Voting and Absence from Meetings," *Yale Law Journal* 209 (1961); also in Leo Gross, *Selected Essays on International Laws and Organization* (New York: Transnational Publishers, 1993) 201.

8. Advisory Opinion of 21 June 1971, Legal Consequences for States of the Continued Presence of South Africa in Namibia (South West Africa) Notwithstanding Security Council Resolution 276 (1970), in 10 ILM 677 sq., esp. paragraphs 113-16 (pp 711-12) in which the Court rather glibly asserts that "decisions" in the sense of Article 25 of the Charter can be made by the Security Council by viewing in full context the Council's assertion that it was, in another resolution "*Mindful* of its responsibility to take necessary action to secure strict compliance with the obligations entered into by States Members …" (para. 115). In fact, this language is taken from Resolution 269 (1970); the Security Council actually did nothing to secure that strict compliance other than pass the later Resolution.

9. Article 27.3 of the Charter requires the "concurring votes" of the permanent members, but since 1950 abstentions have not been regarded as foreclosing the authority of the Security Council to adopt substantive decisions. Nine affirmative votes of the 15 members are still required to pass substantive decisions. UN Charter, Article 27.3. See also the article by Gross cited in note 7 above.

10. For example, the 10 December 1948 Universal Declaration of Human Rights is UN General Assembly Resolution 217 (III). The UN Charter does not give the General Assembly the authority to pass resolutions that bind states members of the organization except with regard to some internal matters, such as the budget, admission to membership in the organization, and so on; human rights are not included in this list.

11. The Council of Europe's Human Rights Convention of 4 November 1950 is one of those, but the parties are only the ratifying states, and to be eligible to ratify the Convention, a state must be a member of the Council of Europe.

12. International Convention on the Elimination of All Forms of Racial Discrimination, 21 December 1965, 660 UNTS 195. This Convention has over 100 parties, including Rwanda, where racial discrimination ultimately reached a point of massive slaughter based on tribal identities, and India, where "untouchable" castes still exist as a matter of social practice and custom, even if not as a matter of other forms of positive law. Another oft-cited example is the Genocide Convention of 9 December 1948, 78 UNTS 277.

13. Article 2.1(c).

14. Articles 8 and 14. The quoted language is from Article 14.

15. 14 ILM 1292 (1975). The provisions on "follow-up" specifically deny that the Act is a Treaty, and undertake (but not in any way that binds legally, only morally) to continue the multilateral process by "a thorough exchange of views on the implementation of the provisions of the Final Act …," presumably allowing any state involved to question the "implementation" of the provisions of the Act by any other state involved; at least that is how it has been interpreted at follow-up conferences. The quoted language appears in 14 ILM at pp. 1324 and 1325.

16. 12 August 1949, Geneva Conventions for the Amelioration of the Condition of the Wounded and Sick in Armed Forces in the Field; for the Amelioration of the Condition of the Wounded, Sick, and Shipwrecked Members of Armed Forces at Sea; Relative to the Treatment of Prisoners of War; and Relative to the Protection of Civilian Persons in Time of War, 75 UNTS 32, 85, 135, and 287 respectively.

17. The language in quotations was taken from Article 146 of the "Civilians" Convention, but there is identical language in all four Geneva Conventions of 1949.

18. See, e.g., the fuss over whether the destruction by explosive device of an American civil aircraft over Lockerbie, Scotland, some years before the Security Council acted in the matter was such a threat when the Security Council acted. Alfred P. Rubin, "Libya, Lockerbie, and the Law," *Diplomacy and Statecraft* 4 (1993): 1-19. That such self-serving declarations have become routine and seem to be accepted by non-involved states is a theme of Mary Ellen O'Connell, "The UN, NATO, and International Law after Kosovo," *Human Rights Quarterly* 22 (2000): 57-89. Whether the non-objection by non-involved states reflects a silent concurrence and thus a disguised revision of the Charter or is just another example of the strength of the inhibition on states intervening in matters where they have no legal interest, no "standing," is a matter about which scholars and diplomats must disagree.

19. Michael P. Malloy, *Economic Sanctions and US Trade* (Boston: Little, Brown, 1990) outlines the entire range of US economic sanctions against the apartheid regime of South Africa in his Chapter 8 (443-97).

20. "CoCom" was the "Coordinating Committee" of NATO allies plus Japan, which exchanged information on exports to listed Communist countries in an attempt to limit involvement in them. It was authorized in the US by 50 USC. app. §2404(i). See Malloy 431.

21. Thomas Jefferson, *Notes on Virginia*, Q. 18 (1785).

7

From Nuremberg to Kosovo: The Morality of Illegal International Legal Reform

Allen Buchanan

The Problem of Illegal Reform

OPTIMISM ABOUT PRACTICE AND IN THEORY

Most would agree that the international legal system has undergone significant moral improvement since 1945. The veil of sovereignty has been pierced: A burgeoning human rights law affirms that how a state treats its own population is no longer its own business only. Slavery, genocide, and aggressive war are prohibited. More states than ever before are democratic. Some scholars even argue that international law is moving toward recognition of a right to democratic governance as a human right.[1] The pro-democracy intervention in Haiti, the expulsion of Iraqi forces from Kuwait, and the NATO intervention in Kosovo have all been praised as valuable steps toward an international system that takes as primary the protection of the rights of individuals rather than the interests of states. Widely discussed goals for further improvement include better compliance with human rights norms; a more consistent, effective, and morally defensible international legal response to secession and other self-determination conflicts; more effective support for democracy; impartial and effective procedures for the prosecution of war crimes; and greater equality among states as actors in the creation and application of international law. The spate of normative writings on secession, self-determination, humanitarian intervention, and on the hypothesis that democratic states do not make war on one another indicates both approval for progress already achieved and the expectation of more progress to come.[2]

LAWLESSNESS IN THE NAME OF PROGRESS

Yet what some hail as progress others decry as illegal acts that threaten the rule of law, betray a lack of sincerity regarding fidelity to law, and manifest a disturbing willingness to impose subjective, personal moral standards on others. To take only two prominent examples, international legal scholars J.S. Watson and Alfred Rubin condemn humanitarian intervention and attempts to enforce human rights norms through the operation of international war crimes tribunals as illegal acts parading under the guise of legality.[3] In addition, they suggest that the source of the illegal reformist's error may lie in his willingness to impose his own subjective view of what morality requires upon others. Such allegations raise a fundamental issue of much greater generality and import than debates over the legal status or the desirability of any particular change in the international legal rules. Under what conditions, if any, is it morally justifiable to engage in acts that violate existing international law in order to bring about supposed moral improvements in the system of international law?

DISTINGUISHING ILLEGAL ACTS OF LEGAL REFORM
FROM MERE CONSCIENTIOUS LAW-BREAKING

Notice that this question is not the same as "Under what conditions, if any, is it morally justifiable to violate international law?" The case of NATO intervention in Kosovo illustrates the distinction. The chief justification US and NATO officials gave for the intervention was that it was necessary to prevent a humanitarian disaster — to stop the massive human rights violations perpetrated by Serbs upon Kosovar Albanians. It appears that the preponderance of international legal opinion is that the intervention was illegal, and it is revealing that US State Department officials were told to avoid the issue of legality in their public statements, presumably because it would be impossible to make a convincing case that the intervention was legal.

In addition to this chief justification, there was the suggestion, on the part of some leaders, including US Secretary of State Madeleine Albright, that the NATO intervention was a first important step toward establishing a new customary norm of international law, according to which humanitarian intervention can be permissible without Security Council authorization. According to this second line of justification, violating existing law was justified to initiate an improvement in the international legal system.

The chief justification presents the illegal action as a necessary exception to law-abidingness in the name of justice, without in anyway implying that the system as a whole, or even the particular rule that is violated, is in need of improvement. Employing this justification is fully consistent with believing that the existing rule that requires Security Council authorization for humanitarian intervention is a good rule, even that it is the best rule possible. The second justification is quite different. It justifies the illegal intervention as an act directed toward reforming the system. Its implication is that the existing rule requiring Security Council authorization is not optimal and that a new norm of humanitarian intervention, according to which Security Council authorization is not needed, is morally preferable.

There is a further difference: an agent who invokes the first justification need not have any commitment to the rule of law; he might, for example, be an anarchist. In contrast, a person who breaks the law with the aim of improving the legal system thereby shows that he values the contribution that a system of law can make to justice. So illegal acts directed toward legal reform are of special interest because, on the one hand, they seem more respectable by virtue of being directed toward improving the system (unlike acts that evidence a total disregard for the rule of law) while, on the other hand, they raise the question of how those who are committed to the rule of law can be willing to break the law. Because my concern in this paper is with the justification of illegal acts directed toward the moral improvement of the international legal system, not with the question of when it is morally justifiable to break the law, I will not canvass the voluminous literature on the obligation to obey the law (and which has focused on domestic law) and then try to determine to what extent its results apply to the case of international law.

Answering the question of when, if ever, illegal acts directed toward improving the international legal system are morally justified is a contribution to the nonideal moral theory of international law. Ideal theory prescribes and justifies the most fundamental principles that an international legal order ought to satisfy. Nonideal theory includes two parts—principles for dealing with noncompliance with the prescriptions of ideal theory and principles for determining the morally accessible ways of making the transition from our nonideal state to a satisfaction of the ideal theory's prescriptions. It is the second part of nonideal theory that includes our question.

DISTINGUISHING ILLEGAL ACTS OF INTERNATIONAL LEGAL REFORM FROM THE STANDARD CASE OF CIVIL DISOBEDIENCE

At this point one might well ask: why restrict the question to *international* law? As the considerable normative literature on civil disobedience shows, the morality of illegal acts for the sake of improving a legal system is hardly a new topic and has been explored thoroughly in regard to domestic legal systems. (For example, Dr. Martin Luther King, Jr. broke state segregation laws to stimulate legislators and the courts to eliminate them and thus make the system of law more just.) Nevertheless, for three reasons the question has particular bite in the case of international law.

First, the illegal acts that are most likely to contribute to the moral improvement of the international legal system differ markedly from acts of civil disobedience, at least when the latter are most clearly morally justifiable. From the standpoint of moral justification, the least problematic case of civil disobedience is that in which the law-breaker violates the law openly and accepts the predictable legal penalty for his act, thus showing respect for law at the same time he violates a particular law. But as I shall elaborate below, in the typical case illegal acts directed toward reform of the international legal system are perpetrated by actors who will not be subject to legal penalty, not simply because the international legal system is weak in enforcement capacity, but because the law-breaker will tend to be a powerful state or coalition against whom punitive action is not likely to be taken.[4]

Second and more important, compared to the better specimens of developed legal systems, the international legal system is both more in need of improvement and less endowed with resources for relatively expeditious lawful improvement. Therefore the question of the morality of illegal acts directed toward system reform is more likely to be more acute and to arise more frequently in the international case.

Third, the illegal acts we are concerned with are not committed by private individuals or groups of private individuals as in the case of civil disobedience; they are state actions, and this raises the stakes of the decision to act illegally. Illegal acts committed by states are, other things being equal, more of a threat to the perceived legitimacy of the system than those committed by private individuals.

The sort of illegal reformist act I shall focus on is exemplified by the NATO action in Kosovo: an illegal act of humanitarian intervention, justified as a contribution toward making the international legal system better from a moral point of view. However, the fundamental question this paper addresses is both wider and narrower than that of the justification of humanitarian intervention: wider, because although the examples I discuss are illegal acts of humanitarian intervention my broader concern is with the more general class of illegal acts directed toward legal reform; narrower, because it is only illegal acts *directed toward legal reform* that I explore and not all acts of humanitarian intervention fit this description.[5]

LIMITED RESOURCES FOR LAWFUL MORAL IMPROVEMENT

The ways in which international law can be made significantly limit the options for lawful reform of the system. There are two chief sources of international law: treaty and custom. If the target of moral improvement is to prohibit a form of behavior engaged in by more than a few states or to create a new norm that allows behavior that previously would have been a violation of the rights of sovereignty that all states enjoy, reform by treaty may be a very slow process at best. Suppose that the goal of reform is to establish a norm of international law that not only requires states to "promote" human rights within their own borders and to supply periodic reports on their progress in doing so to some international body (as the major human rights covenants stipulate), but that also authorizes armed intervention to halt massive human rights violations that occur in domestic conflicts when less intrusive means have failed. Many states will refuse to sign such a treaty. Others may sign but postpone ratification indefinitely. Others may sign and ratify, but weaken the force of the document by stating "reservations" regarding some clauses (thereby exempting themselves from their requirements) or by stating "understandings" which interpret burdensome clauses in ways that make them less threatening to state interests.

As an avenue for moral improvements that are both significant and timely, the process by which international customary law is formed is hardly more promising. In briefest terms, new norms of customary law are created as the result of the emergence of a persistent pattern of behavior by states, accompanied by the belief that the behavior in question is legally required or authorized (the *opinio juris* condition). However, there are several aspects of this process that significantly limit the efficacy of the customary route toward system improvement. First, international law allows states to opt out of the new customary norm's scope by consistently dissenting from them. Second, how widespread the new pattern of state behavior must be before a new norm can be said to have "crystallized" is not only disputed, but probably not capable of a definitive answer. Third, even if a sufficiently widespread and persisting pattern of behavior is established, the satisfaction of the *opinio juris* condition may be less clear and more subject to dispute. Pronouncements by state leaders may be ambiguous or mixed, in some cases indicating a recognition of the behavior in question as legally required or authorized, in other cases appearing to deny it.

Given these limitations, the efforts of the state or states that first attempt to initiate the process of customary change are fraught with uncertainty. Particularly if the new norm they seek to establish addresses a long-standing and widespread pattern of state behavior, and one in which many states profess to be legally entitled to persist, other states may not follow suit. Or, if other states follow suit, they may do so for strictly pragmatic reasons and may attempt to ensure that a new customary rule does not emerge by officially registering that they do not regard their behavior as legally required (thus thwarting satisfaction of the *opinio juris* condition).

The crucial point is that new customary norms do not emerge from a single action or even from a persistent pattern of action by one state or a small group of states. Thus, the initial effort to create a new customary norm is a gamble. A new norm is created only when the initial behavior is repeated consistently by a preponderance of states over a considerable period of time and only when there is a shift in the legal consciousness of all or most states as to what the law is. At any point the process can break down. For example, if one powerful state dissents from an emerging norm, other states may decide that it is prudent to register dissent as well or to refrain from pronouncements that would otherwise count as evidence for satisfaction of the *opinio juris* requirement. For all of these reasons, significant and timely reform through the creation of new customary norms of international law is difficult and uncertain.

That reliance on change through the establishment of new custom is a formidable obstacle to fundamental social change has long been recognized. All of the great proponents of the modern state—the state with legislative sovereignty—from Bodin and Hobbes to Rousseau, recognized the severe limitations that adherence to the evolution of customary law imposed on the possibilities for reform. Only the power to issue and enforce rules that can overturn even the most deeply entrenched customary norms in domestic society would suffice; thus, the insistence on legislative sovereignty. But in the international legal system there is as yet nothing approaching a universal legislature. Nor is there a process of constitutional amendment. To summarize: heavy reliance on customary law, absence of both a universal legislature capable of overturning custom and a constitutional amendment process, and the obvious limitations of the treaty process, together result in a system in which lawful reform is more difficult than in developed domestic systems.[6]

Although they are quite different mechanisms for the creation of international law, treaty and custom have this in common: they both rely heavily on states' acceptance of norms as binding. Indeed, the idea that state consent (whether explicit, as in the case of treaties, or tacit, as with custom) is essential is the predominant view of what is distinctive of international law. There are well-known difficulties in the idea that customary norms enjoy the consent of all states (in particular, not opting out cannot properly be regarded as tacitly consenting), and there is also the problem that international law counts as consensual agreements that are far from voluntary on the part of one party (peace treaties signed under duress by the losers in war are said to be consented to by them). Nevertheless, there is a substantial kernel of truth in the assertion that the system exists through state consent. The mechanisms of treaty and custom result in a system in which it is extremely difficult for anyone to impose norms which the majority of states oppose.

This broadly consensual nature of international law undoubtedly brings some benefits. For example, it may make it more difficult for a hegemon to hijack the international legal system for its own purposes. Nonetheless, what might be loosely called the state consent super-norm comes at a steep price: it makes timely moral reform difficult in a system which few would deny needs improvement.

LAWLESSNESS AS A NECESSARY ELEMENT IN
THE EMERGENCE OF NEW CUSTOMARY NORMS

Suppose that a state decides to try to initiate the process by which a new customary norm may emerge. Suppose that the new norm the state is trying to help to bring into existence addresses a long-standing and widespread pattern of wrongful state behavior, one in which many states profess to be entitled to persist in as falling within the proper scope of their sovereign rights. The first acts that a state performs hoping to initiate the process of creating the new norm will be illegal—they will violate the existing norms concerning the scope of sovereignty. Yet only if such illegal acts are performed can change through the emergence of new customary norms occur. Later I will explore the question of how the moral justification of illegal acts of reform is effected by the fact that changes in customary law essentially involves illegality.

ILLEGAL ACTS DIRECTED TOWARD SYSTEM REFORM: THREE EXAMPLES

To clarify what is at stake in the issue of the morality of illegal legal reform, consider the following hypothetical cases.

Case 1: Bowing to sustained international pressure, Iraq agrees to grant autonomy (limited self-government, not full independence) to the Kurdish people in its northern region. But, as with its 1970 autonomy regime for the Kurds, Iraq violates the agreement. A multinational force "endorsed" by a UN General Assembly Resolution but not empowered by a decision of the Security Council, intervenes to restore the Kurd's autonomy and to create a monitoring mechanism to provide early warning if Iraq seeks to violate the autonomy arrangement in the future.

Case 2: A new genocide erupts in Burundi. A coalition of French and American forces quickly intervenes, disarms the perpetrators of genocide, arrests their leaders, and turns them over to an international genocide tribunal. Neither the Secretary General of the UN, nor the Security Council, nor the General Assembly endorse this intervention, but they do not condemn it either.

Case 3: A small Latin American country has just achieved its first truly democratic election. But then a group of fascist colonels in its armed forces overthrows the newly elected government by force and "permanently abolish-es" democracy. A coalition of key members of the Organization of American States intervenes militarily and restores the elected government.

Were these events to occur there is little doubt that many members of the general public and perhaps a majority of international legal theorists would view at least some of them favorably, as contributions toward a more morally sound international order in which human rights and democracy are better protected than at present. No doubt some theorists would portray these events as the first hopeful steps toward establishing new, more morally enlightened norms of international customary law. They would hope that these types of actions would be repeated and that eventually new norms would crystallize.

PERMISSIVE VERSUS OBLIGATORY NORMS

These examples indicate another feature of the process of customary norm creation. The same type of behavior (for example, intervention to prevent genocide, as in case 2) might exemplify the content of either a permissive or an obligatory norm of intervention. In the former case, the new customary norm would be established only after the emergence of a sustained pattern of intervention, accompanied by the belief that the intervention was legally permissible under international law; in the latter, it would be established only if the pattern of behavior were accompanied by the belief that intervening is obligatory. Presumably, as a broad generalization, the establishment of a new permissive customary norm should be less difficult, to the extent that it does not impose affirmative duties on states, but only increases the scope of their lawful discretionary action and in that sense does not represent a radical change in a system that has traditionally left much to the decisions of states. However, this generalization is subject to an important exception: if the new permissive norm in effect cancels a pre-existing prohibition against noncon-sensual action toward other states, as is the case with a permissive norm of humanitarian intervention, then it represents a very significant change and one which states may resist.

CHANGING SECONDARY RULES BY CHANGING PRIMARY RULES

Hart draws a distinction between primary rules, which make certain behaviors permissible or obligatory, and secondary rules, which specify how primary rules may be changed.[7] So far I have considered the possibility of illegal acts performed with the aim of creating new primary customary norms, such as either a permissive or an obligatory norm of humanitarian intervention. However, it is conceivable that if such illegal acts of reform occurred repeatedly and succeeded in initiating processes by which a number of new primary norms actually emerged, a more fundamental change in the system would occur. A new secondary rule that law can be created without state consent, and hence a challenge to the traditional conception of the international legal system, might arise. If this were to occur, the sorts of acts that are now considered illegal, in particular those involving nonconsensual incursion into what are now regarded as the internal affairs of states, might then become legal, according to the new secondary rule. But whether this sort of change would constitute moral progress or would instead make the system less morally defensible by making it easier for stronger states to oppress weaker ones or for ideology-driven states to impose their own subjective moral views on others, is an important question.

It follows that the process of providing a moral justification for an illegal act of reform may be quite complex. It may not be sufficient to make a case that the new primary rule that the agent is trying to help establish is sufficiently progressive to warrant an illegal act on the assumption that the only change will be an alteration of the primary rules; it may also be necessary to argue that the illegal act is not likely to undermine a secondary rule that ought to be preserved.

AVOIDING THE "WHAT IS LAW?" QUESTION

My aim in articulating the three examples above is not to take a firm position on the question of whether any particular effort to improve the international legal system is illegal. I believe that it is relatively uncontroversial that in at least some of the three cases, if not all three, the act in question would be deemed uncontroversial by the preponderance of experts in international law. The choice of particular examples is not important, however. The key point is this: given the relatively undeveloped state of international law—in particular its inadequate protection of basic human rights and its limited resources for timely and lawful change in the direction of more adequate protection—there are opportunities for acts which are both illegal and highly desirable as steps toward morally improving the system. To raise the question of the morality of illegal international legal reform, we need not agree on a definitive and comprehensive solution to the hoary question, "what is international law?" or "when is a norm an international law?"

FACING THE QUESTION OF ILLEGAL ACTS OF REFORM SQUARELY

Critics such as Watson and Rubin are right to suggest that too often those who endorse what they regard as acts of reform evade the question of whether illegal acts are morally justifiable by assuming, without good reason, that the acts in question are not really illegal.[8] Without resolving complex debates about what the law is, I wish to confront head-on the question of whether and, if so, under what conditions illegal acts of reform are morally justified.

Now it might be objected at this juncture that in spite of the fact that international law lacks some of the powerful resources for lawful moral reform available in developed domestic systems (such as a supreme legislature and a constitutional amendment process), international law has achieved remarkable moral progress in only 50 years. Given that this is so, there is reason for optimism that further major improvements can be made without illegality.

My reply is that some of the most important moral improvements in the international legal system have resulted, at least in part, from illegal acts. Consider one of the great landmarks of reform: the outlawing of genocide. To a large extent this was an achievement of the Nuremberg War Crimes Tribunal (though at the time the term "genocide" was not part of the legal lexicon). However, a strong case has been made by a number of respected commentators that the "Victors' Justice" at Nuremberg was illegal under existing international law. In particular, it has been argued that there was no customary norm or treaty prohibiting what the Tribunal called "crimes against humanity" at the time World War II occurred. But quite apart from this it has been argued that even if (contrary to what some commentators say) aggressive war was prohibited at the time the war began, there was no international law authorizing the criminal prosecution of individuals for waging or conspiring to wage aggressive war.

There is no denying that the Nuremberg Tribunal contributed to some of the changes in international law that we regard as the epitome of progress — not just the prohibitions of genocide and aggressive war, but also the international recognition of the rights of human subjects of medical experimentation.[9] Nonetheless, a strong case can be made that at least some, if not all, of the punishments meted out at Nuremberg were probably illegal.

It can also be argued that a series of illegal actions over several decades played a significant role in one of the other most admirable improvements in the international legal system: the prohibition of slavery. In the late eighteenth and early nineteenth centuries Britain used the unrivalled power of its navy to attack the transatlantic slave trade.[10] Britain's strategy included illegal searches and seizures of ships flying under other nations' flags, as well as attempts to get other countries to enforce their own laws against commerce in human beings. It is highly probable that what success Britain had in persuading other states to cooperate in efforts to destroy the slave trade was due in part to its willingness to use illegal force. The destruction of the slave trade was a milestone in the development of a growing human rights movement that eventually issued in the international legal prohibition of slavery, but which also expanded to include other human rights.

Once the pivotal role of such illegal acts is acknowledged, it is unconvincing to appeal to the moral progress that has already been achieved in international law to support the assumption that significant continued progress will be achieved with reasonable speed and without illegality. On the contrary, given the system's limited resources for lawful change—and the fact that it is still a state-dominated system in which many of the most serious defects calling for reform lie in the behavior of states—the question of the morality of illegal reform is inescapable.

The Condemnation of Illegal Reform Efforts

We can now proceed to evaluate the position of those, such as Watson and Rubin, who condemn what they take to be illegal acts done in the name of the moral improvement of the international legal system. Such critics raise an issue that is as fundamental as it is neglected: under what conditions, if any, is it morally justifiable to breach international law in order to try to improve the system from a moral point of view? To answer this question, I shall argue, we must answer two others: (1) what is the moral basis of the commitment to bringing international relations under the rule of law? And (2) under what conditions, if any, can an agent's judgments about what justice requires count as good reasons for imposing rules on others? In order to answer question (1) we need an account of *fidelity to law* that enables us to determine how the would-be reformer should weigh the fact that his proposed action of reform is illegal. In order to answer question (2) we need an account of *moral authority* (or what Rawls calls legitimacy) that enables us to determine if the would-be reformer is justified imposing on others a norm to which they have not consented and which some would reject. A satisfactory answer to the first question is needed to counter the charge that advocates of illegal acts directed toward system reform show lack of due respect for law while purporting to improve it. A satisfactory answer to the second question is needed to refute the allegation that advocates of illegal acts directed toward system reform are wrongly seeking to impose their own "subjective" moral views on others. I will address the issue of fidelity to law in the next section and the issue of moral authority later in this paper.

Unfortunately, critics like Watson and Rubin have done a better job of raising the issue of the morality of illegal legal reform than of resolving it. It is fair to say that both authors assume, more than argue, that illegalities in the name of system reform are not morally justified. At the very least, the exact character of their complaint is not clear. It is possible to begin the task of appreciating the condemnation of illegal acts of reform by reconstructing a simple argument on their behalf. Call it the Fidelity Argument. It purports to explain why the fact that the reformist's act is illegal counts decisively against the morality of the act.

1. One ought to be committed to the rule of law in international relations.

2. If one is committed to the rule of law in international relations, then one cannot consistently advocate (what one recognizes to be) illegal acts as a means of morally improving the system of international law.

3. Therefore, one ought not to advocate illegal acts as a means of morally improving the system of international law.

Bases for Fidelity to Law

Those who condemn illegal acts of reform often present themselves as no-nonsense legal positivists, suggesting that those who endorse illegal acts of reform are typically extreme naturalists who confuse their own assumptions about how law ought to be with the facts about what the law is.[11] It might be argued, however, that it is the critics of illegal reform who are insufficiently positivistic, at least so far as the creation of new custom is concerned, for as we have already seen changes in customary law *require* illegality (when the first acts or omissions that contribute to a new custom violate existing custom). Given that this is the case, illegality is a necessary feature of *this* sort of legal system, and hence is compatible with *its* rule of law. In other words, critics such as Rubin and Watson can be accused of ignoring the actual character of the international legal system and basing their condemnation of illegal acts of reform on their own personal assumptions about how a legal system ought to be.[12]

I do not take this ad hominem to be a sufficient answer to the question of whether illegal acts of moral reform are morally justifiable. For one thing, even if it is accurate to say that the international legal system's secondary rules regarding the creation of new customary norms in effect authorizes illegality, the moral question remains: when ought an agent to utilize this mechanism for change? However, I do believe that the ad hominem argument at least helps to motivate scrutiny of the critics' assumption that respect for the rule of law and illegal acts of reform are necessarily incompatible in the case of the international legal system. To do so we must evaluate the Fidelity Argument.

The first step is to clarify the phrase "the rule of law" in the argument in order to understand just why honoring the commitment to the rule of law is important. There are in fact two quite different ways in which critics of illegal reform may be understanding "the rule of law" in the Fidelity Argument. According to the first, "the rule of law" refers to a normatively rich ideal for systems of rules. According to the second, it means something that may be much less normatively demanding, namely, a system of rules capable of preventing a Hobbesian condition of violent chaos. Let us see how the Fidelity Argument reads under these two interpretations.

FIDELITY TO THE IDEAL OF LAW

According to the first interpretation, the rule of law is an ideal composed of several elements: laws are to be general, public, not subject to frequent or arbitrary changes, and their requirements must be reasonably clear and such that human beings of normal capacities are able to comply with them.[13] These requirements help ensure that a system of law provides a stable framework of expectations, so that individuals can plan their projects with some confidence and coordinate their behavior with that of others. But there is another element of the rule of law as a normative ideal which on some accounts is of signal importance: the requirement of equality before the law. The precise import of this requirement is, of course, subject to much dispute, but the core idea is that the law is to be applied and enforced impartially.

If we read "the rule of law" in the Fidelity Argument as referring to this normatively demanding ideal—as including the requirement of equality before the law—then the argument is subject to a serious and obvious objection. The difficulty is that the international legal system falls short of the requirement of equality before the law. The most powerful states (such as China, the US, and the Russian Federation) not only play an arbitrarily disproportionate role in the processes by which international law is made and applied, but are also often able to violate the law with impunity.

According to the first interpretation of the Fidelity Argument, it is our moral allegiance to the rule of law as a normative ideal that is supposed to be inconsistent with advocating or committing what we believe to be illegal acts even if they are directed toward reforming the system. But to the extent that the existing system falls far short of the ideal of the rule of law in one of its most fundamental elements, the requirement of equality before the law, allegiance to the ideal exerts less moral pull toward strict fidelity to its rules. Indeed, allegiance to the rule of law as an ideal might be thought to make illegal acts *morally obligatory* in a system that does a very poor job of approximating the requirements of the ideal. More specifically, a sincere commitment to the rule of law might be a powerful reason for committing illegal acts directed toward bringing the system closer to fulfillment of the requirement of equality before the law, if there is no lawful way to achieve this reform.[14] The point is that one cannot move directly from the commitment to the rule of law as an ideal to strict fidelity to existing law. Whether a commitment to the rule of law as an ideal precludes illegal reform actions will depend in part upon the extent to which the existing system approximates the ideal.

Notice also that the critics' second complaint has little force against illegal acts of reform directed toward making the system better satisfy the requirements of the ideal of the rule of law, especially that of equality before the law. To say that the core accepted elements of the rule of law are merely the personal moral views of the reformers, and that it would therefore be illegitimate to impose them on others, would be extremely inaccurate. Not only are they widely accepted, but unless they are assumed to be highly desirable it is hard to make sense of the idea of fidelity to the law as a moral ideal. In the next section we will see that the illegitimacy issue — the question of when an agent is morally justified in imposing moral standards on those who do not accept them — has more bite when the moral principles motivating illegal acts of reform are more controversial.

SUBSTANTIVE JUSTICE

There is another reason why a simple appeal to the ideal of the rule of law cannot show that illegal reform acts are not morally justifiable: the extent to which a system of rules exemplifies the ideal of the rule of law is not the only factor that determines the moral pull toward compliance. Approximation of the ideal of the rule of law is a necessary, not a sufficient, condition for our being obligated to comply with legal norms, even if a deep commitment to the ideal of the rule of law is assumed. A system might do a reasonably good job of exemplifying the elements of the rule of law and still be seriously defective from the standpoint of substantive principles of justice. For example, the system might be compatible with, or even promote, unjust economic inequalities, depending upon the content of the laws of property and the extent to which the current distribution of wealth is the result of past injustices. Similarly, the elements of the ideal might be satisfied, or at least closely approximated, in a system that failed to meet even the most minimal standards of democratic participation. The elements of the rule of law prevent certain kinds of injustices and help ensure the stability and predictability that rational agents need, but this is not to say that they capture the whole of justice. And if justice is to enjoy the kind of moral priority that is widely thought to be essential to its very notion, then one cannot assume that illegal acts directed toward eliminating grave injustice in the system are always ruled out by fidelity to the ideal of the rule of law. Since many, indeed perhaps most, extant theories of justice include more than the requirements of the rule of law, it would be very misleading to assume that any illegal action for the sake of reforming the international legal system by making it more just must be the imposition of the reformer's subjective view of morality or merely personal views.

Nevertheless, a more subtle form of the legitimacy issue remains. Even if it is true that most or even all understandings of justice take it to include more than an approximation of the ideal of the rule of law, there is much disagreement about what justice requires, and it is appropriate to ask what makes it morally justifiable for an actor to try to impose on others the conception of justice she endorses. I take up the moral authority issue in the next section.

Earlier I suggested that an approximate conception of the ideal of the rule of law would include the requirement of equality before the law. Some might disagree, limiting the ideal of the rule of law to the other elements listed above. If they are right, then this is further confirmation that the rule of law is not the only value that is relevant to assessing the weight of our commitment to fidelity to law. If equality before the law is not to be included in the ideal of the rule of law, then there is a strong case for including it among the most basic and least controversial principles of justice, at least for those who value the role that law can play in securing justice. But if so, then whether it is morally permissible to violate a law to improve a legal system must surely depend in part on how unjust the system is.

THE LEGITIMACY OF THE INTERNATIONAL LEGAL SYSTEM

The international legal system not only tolerates extreme economic inequalities among individuals and among states; it legitimizes and stabilizes them in manifold ways, not the least of which is by supporting state sovereignty over resources.[15] In addition, it is characterized by extreme political inequality among the primary members of the system (states). As already noted, a handful of powerful states wield a disproportionate influence over the creation and, above all, the application and enforcement of international law. Indeed, it is not implausible to argue that the extreme and morally arbitrary political inequality that characterizes the society of formally equal states robs the system of legitimacy. By a legitimate system I mean one whose institutional structures provide a framework within which its authorized actors are morally justified in making, applying, and enforcing laws.

To make a convincing case that these defects deprive the international legal system of legitimacy would require articulating and defending a theory of system legitimacy.[16] That task lies far beyond the scope of the present discussion. However, this much can be said: the more problematic a system's claim to legitimacy, the weaker the moral pull of fidelity to its laws, other things being equal. Neither Watson or Rubin address the issue of whether illegal acts of reform may be justified if they hold a reasonable prospect of significantly improving the legitimacy of a system whose legitimacy is at the very least subject to doubt. However, we shall see later that there is a way of understanding their opposition to illegal reform as resting on a conception of system legitimacy that emphasizes adherence to the state consent super-norm.

Given the existing international legal system's deficiencies from the standpoint of what is either a cardinal element of the ideal of the rule of law or a basic, widely shared principle of justice, namely, equality before the law, and from the standpoint of a fairly wide range of principles of distributive justice, and given that the extreme political inequality among the states poses a serious challenge to the legitimacy of the system, it is implausible to assert that a commitment to the rule of law, as a moral ideal, rules out all illegal action for the sake of reform. The very defects of the system that provide the most obvious targets for reform weaken the moral pull of strict fidelity to its laws.

So far my analysis only shows that there is no simple inference from allegiance to the ideal of the rule of law to the moral unjustifiability of illegal acts directed to system reform. It does not follow, of course, that everything is morally permissible in a system as defective as the international legal system so long as it is done in the name of reforming the system. An important question remains: given that a commitment to the ideal of the rule of law does not categorically prohibit illegal acts of reform, under what conditions are which sorts of illegal acts of reform morally justified? As a first approximation of an answer, we can say that, other things being equal, illegal acts are more readily justified if they have a reasonable prospect of contributing toward (a) bringing the system significantly closer to the ideal of the rule of law in its most fundamental elements, (b) rectifying the most serious substantive injustices supported by the system, or (c) ameliorating defects in the system that impugn its legitimacy.

THE RULE OF LAW AS NECESSARY FOR AVOIDING VIOLENT CHAOS

Our first interpretation of the rule of law in the Fidelity Argument understood that phrase in a normatively demanding way: To be committed to the rule of law is to respect and endeavor to promote systems of rules that satisfy or seriously approximate a robust conception of the quality of law. We saw that on this interpretation the connection between being committed to the rule of law and refusing to violate existing international law is more tenuous and conditional than the critics of illegal reform assume. The second interpretation of the rule of law as it occurs in the Fidelity Argument owes more to Hobbes than to Fuller. The idea is that even if international law falls far short of exemplifying some of the key elements of the ideal of the rule of law and even if it is seriously deficient from the standpoint of substantive justice and legitimacy, it is all that stands between us and violent chaos.[17] On this interpretation of the Fidelity Argument, we are presented with an austere choice: abstaining from illegal acts of reform or risking a Hobbesian war of each against all in international relations.

This is a false dilemma. As a sweeping generalization, the claim that illegal acts of reform run an unconscionable risk of violent anarchy is implausible. It would be more plausible if two assumptions were true: (a) the existence of the international order depends solely upon the efficacy of international law; and (b) international law is a seamless web, so that cutting one fiber (violating one norm) will result in the unraveling of the entire fabric.

The first assumption is dubious. It probably overestimates the role of law by underestimating the contributions of political and economic relations and the various institutions of transnational civil society to peace and stability in international relations. But even if the first assumption were justified, the second, "seamless web" assumption is far-fetched. History refutes it. As we have already noted, there have been illegal acts that were directed toward and that actually contributed to significant reforms, yet they did not result in a collapse of the international legal system.

RESPECT FOR THE STATE CONSENT SUPER-NORM

Some critics of illegal reform, including Watson and Rubin, are especially troubled by the willingness of reformers to violate what these critics believe is an essential (constitutional) feature of the existing international legal system: the state consent super-norm, a secondary rule according to which law is to be made and changed only by the consent of states.[18] (As was noted earlier, the requirement of state consent here is understood in a very loose way to be satisfied either by ratification of treaties or through conformity to norms that achieve the status of customary law.) The question, then, is this: why is the state consent super-norm of such importance that illegal acts of reform that violate it are never morally justified? There appear to be three answers worth considering: (1) only if the state consent super-norm is strictly observed will violent chaos be avoided, because only state consent can render international law *effective*; (2) state consent is the only mechanism for creating effective norms of peaceful relations among states that is capable of conferring *legitimacy* upon international norms; or (3) the state consent super-norm ought to be strictly adhered to because doing so reduces the risk that stronger states will prey on weaker ones.

1. The general claim that compliance with legal norms can only be achieved if those whose behavior is regulated by the norms consent to them is clearly false. In the case of domestic legal systems, virtually no one would assert that consent to every norm is necessary for effectiveness. So if the importance of consent is to supply a decisive reason against acts of reform that violate the state consent super-norm in international law, it must be because there is something special about the international arena that makes consent necessary if law is to be effective enough to avoid violent chaos.

If the realist theory of international relations were correct, it would provide an answer to the question of what that something special is. According to the realist theory, the structure of international relations precludes moral action except where it happens to be congruent with state interest. The importance of creating norms by state consent, on this view, is that it provides a way for states, understood as purely self-interested actors, to promote their shared long-term interests in peace and stability. Unless realism is correct, it is hard to see why we should assume that consent is necessary for effective law in the international case, while acknowledging, as we must, that it is not necessary for effectiveness in domestic systems.

Realism has been vigorously attacked, most systematically by contributors to the Liberal theory of international relations. Because I believe these attacks are telling, I will not re-enact now all too familiar argumentative battles between realists and their critics. Instead, I will focus on the second and third versions of the argument that a proper appreciation of the consensual basis of existing international law precludes justifiable acts of illegal reform.[19]

2. This is the view that what is morally attractive about the existing international legal system is not just that it avoids the Hobbesian abyss, but that it does so by relying upon the only mechanism for creating and changing norms of peaceful interaction that can confer legitimacy upon norms, given the character of international relations.[20] (A legitimate norm, here, is understood as one that it is morally justifiable to enforce.) The underlying assumption is that the members of the so-called community of states are moral strangers, that rather than a genuine community the state system is a mere association of distinct societies that do not share substantive ends of a conception of justice.[21] In the absence of shared substantive ends or a common conception of justice, consent is the only basis of legitimacy for a system of norms. Within domestic societies, there are moral-political cultures that are "thick" enough to fund shared substantive ends or conceptions of justice and hence to provide a basis for legitimacy without consent; but not so in international "society." But if state consent is the only basis for legitimacy in the international system, then illegal acts of reform that violate the state consent super-norm, such as

illegal interventions to support democracy or to prevent massive violations of human rights in ethnic conflicts within states, strike at the very foundation of international law and hence are not morally justifiable, at least for those who profess to be committed to reforming that system.[22]

The most obvious defect of this line of argument is that its contrast between international society as a collection of moral strangers and domestic society as an ethical community united by a "thick" culture of common values is overdrawn. Especially in liberal societies, which tolerate and even promote pluralism, whatever it is that legitimates the system of legal rules, it cannot be shared substantive ends or even a shared conception of justice. What this thesis overlooks is that democratic politics in liberal domestic societies includes deliberation—and heated controversy—over which substantive ends to pursue, not simply over which means to use to pursue shared substantive ends. In particular, liberal domestic societies often contain deep divisions as to conceptions of distributive justice, with some citizens espousing "welfare-state" conceptions and others "minimal state" or libertarian conceptions. Yet such societies somehow manage to avoid violent chaos and also appear to be capable of having legal systems that are legitimate.

An advocate of this thesis might respond, relying on Rawls's views in *Political Liberalism* and *The Law of Peoples*, that the members of liberal societies do share what might be called a core conception of justice—the idea that society is a cooperative venture among persons conceived as free and equal—but that there is no globally shared core conception of justice. Hence comes their adherence to the state consent super-norm as necessary in international law, but not in domestic law.

There are three difficulties with this response. First, divisions within liberal domestic societies, especially concerning distributive justice, may be so deep that we must conclude either that (a) there is no shared core conception of justice or that (b) if there is it is so vague and elastic that it cannot serve as a foundation for a legitimate system of legal norms. (Even if it is true that welfare state liberals and libertarians both hold that society is a cooperative endeavor among "free and equal" persons, their respective understandings of what freedom and equality are diverge sharply.) Second, and more important, even if it is, or once was true, that value pluralism among states is much deeper than within them, there is evidence that this may be changing. As many commentators have stressed, international legal institutions, as well as the forces of economic globalization, have contributed to the development of a transnational civil society in which a culture of human rights is emerging. This culture of human rights is both founded on and serves to extend a shared conception of basic human interests and a conception of the minimal institutional arrangements needed to protect them.[23] Moreover, the canonical language of the major human rights documents indicates a tendency toward convergence that may be as good a candidate for a core shared conception of justice as that which Rawls attributes to liberal societies: the idea that human beings have an inherent equality and freedom. So even if it is true that a system of legal norms can be legitimate only if it is supported by a common culture of basic values or a shared core conception of justice, it is not clear that international society is so lacking in moral consensus that state consent must remain an indispensable condition if norms are to be legitimate.

There is a third, much more serious objection to the proposition that illegal acts of reform that violate the state consent super-norm are morally unjustifiable because they undermine the only basis for legitimacy in the international legal system: Due to the very defects at which illegal acts of reform are directed, the normative force of state consent in the present system is morally questionable at best.

What is called state consent is really the consent of state leaders. But in the many states in which human rights are massively and routinely violated and where democratic institutions are lacking, state leaders cannot reasonably be regarded as agents of their people.[24] Where human rights are massively violated, individuals are prevented or deterred from participating in processes of representation, consultation, and deliberation that are necessary if state leaders are to function as agents of the people capable of exercising authority on their behalf.

But if state leaders are not agents of their peoples, then it cannot be said that state consent is binding because it expresses the people's will. How, then, can the consent of individuals who cannot reasonably be viewed as agents of the peoples they claim to represent confer legitimacy? Illegal acts directed toward creating the only conditions under which state consent could confer legitimacy cannot be ruled out as morally unjustifiable on the grounds that they violate the norm of state consent.

This is not to say that the requirement of state consent, under present conditions, is without benefit or that the benefits it brings are irrelevant to the question of whether the system is legitimate. It can be argued, as I have already suggested, that adherence to the state consent super-norm has considerable instrumental value, quite apart from the inability of state consent as such to confer legitimacy on norms. This is the point of the third thesis about the importance of the state consent requirement.

3. This third account of why the state consent super-norm is so important as to preclude illegal acts of reform that violate it is much more plausible than the first two. It does not assume that any violation of the norm of state consent poses an unacceptable risk of violent chaos, nor that state consent is supremely

valuable because only it can achieve peace through norms that are legitimate. The proponent of this third thesis can cheerfully admit that law can be effective without consent and that under existing conditions state consent is in itself incapable of conferring legitimacy on the norms consented to. Instead, her point is that adherence to the state consent super-norm is so instrumentally valuable for reducing predation by stronger states upon weaker ones that it ought not to be violated even for the sake of system reform. This thesis relies on the empirical prediction that if the international legal system fails to preserve the formal political equality of states by adhering to the state consent super-norm, the material inequalities among states will result in predatory behavior and in the violations of individual human rights as well as rights of self-determination which predation inevitably entails.[25]

It is no doubt true that the state consent super-norm provides valuable protection for weaker states. But even if this is so, it does not follow that acts of reform that violate the state consent super-norm are never morally justifiable. Acts of reform that are very likely to make a significant contribution to making the system more egalitarian—that contribute to increasing the substantive political equality of states, thereby reducing the risk of predation—may be morally justified under certain circumstances, even if they violate the state consent super-norm.

Another way to put this point is to note that the instrumental argument for strict adherence to the state consent super-norm is very much a creature of nonideal theory. At least from the standpoint of a wide range of theories of distributive justice the existing global distribution of resources and goods is seriously unjust. But presumably these injustices play a major role in the inequalities of power among states. If the system became more distributively just, the inequalities of power that create opportunities for predation would diminish, and with them the threat of predation and the instrumental value of the state consent super-norm.

What this means is that there is nothing inconsistent in both appreciating the value of adherence to the state consent super-norm as a way of reducing predation and being willing to violate it in order to bring about systemic changes that will undercut the conditions for predation. The difficulty for the responsible reformer lies in determining when the prospects for actually achieving a significant reform in the direction of greater equality or justice are good enough to warrant undertaking an action that may have the effect of weakening what may be the best bulwark against predation the system presently possesses. While the instrumental (anti-predation) argument may be powerful enough to create a strong presumption—for the time being—against violating the state consent super-norm, it is hard to see how it can provide a categorical prohibition on illegal acts of reform. Furthermore, observing the state consent super-norm is not the only mechanism for reducing the risk of predation. The theory and practice of constitutionalism in domestic legal systems offer a variety of mechanisms for checking abuses of power. For example, a norm requiring that individual states or groups of states may intervene in domestic conflicts to protect human rights only when explicitly authorized to do so by a supermajority vote in the UN General Assembly would provide a valuable constraint on great power abuses.

The results of this section can now be briefly summarized. I have argued the notion that fidelity to law cannot provide a decisive reason for refraining from committing illegal acts directed toward reforming the international legal system. A sincere commitment to the ideal of the rule of law is not only consistent with illegal acts of reform, it may in some cases make such acts obligatory. Further, it is not plausible to argue that illegal acts of reform always constitute an unacceptable threat to peace and stability. Finally, I have argued that being willing to commit an illegal act of reform need not be inconsistent with a proper appreciation of the need to provide weaker states with protection against predation. I now turn to the other main challenge to illegal international legal reform: the charge that reformers wrongly impose their own personal or subjective views of morality upon others.

Moral Authority

THE CHARGE OF SUBJECTIVISM

Opponents of illegal reform such as Watson and Rubin heap scathing criticism on those who would impose their own personal or subjective views of morality or justice on others. The suggestion is that those who endorse violations of international law, and especially those who disregard the state consent supernorm, are intolerant ideologues who would deny to others the right to do what they do. It is a mistake, however, to assume, as these critics apparently do, that the only alternatives are subjectivism or strict adherence to legality.

INTERNALIST MORAL CRITICISM OF THE SYSTEM

An agent who seeks to breach international law in order to initiate a process of bringing about a moral improvement in the system need not be appealing to a subjective or merely personal view about morality. Instead, she may be relying upon moral values that are already expressed in the system and, to the extent that the system is consensual, upon principles that are widely shared. In fact, it appears that some who were sympathetic to NATO's intervention in Kosovo, including UN Secretary General Kofi Annan, believed that this intervention was supported by one of the most morally defensible fundamental principles of the international legal system, the obligation to protect human rights, even though it was consistent with another principle of the system, the norm of sovereignty understood as prohibiting intervention in the domestic affairs of Serbia-Montenegro.[26] To describe those who supported the intervention by appealing to basic human rights principles internal to the system as ideologues relying on a merely personal or subjective moral view is wildly inaccurate.

TWO VIEWS OF MORAL AUTHORITY

Since the appearance of Rawls's book *Political Liberalism* there has been a complex and spirited debate about the nature of what I have called moral authority. Two main rival views have emerged. According to the first, which Rawls himself offers, moral authority, understood as the right to impose rules on others, is subject to a requirement of reasonableness. It is morally justifiable to impose on others only those principles that they could reasonably accept from the standpoint of their own comprehensive conceptions of the good or of justice, with the proviso that the latter fall within the range of the reasonable.[27] Rawls has a rather undemanding notion of what counts as a reasonable conception of the good or of justice: so long as the view is logically consistent or coherent and includes the idea that every person's good should count in the design of basic social institutions, it counts as reasonable. As I have argued elsewhere, Rawls's conception of moral authority counts as reasonable grossly inegalitarian societies, including those that include systematic, institutionalized racism or caste systems or systems that discriminate systematically against women.[28] The point is that on Rawls's view grossly and arbitrarily inegalitarian social systems count as reasonable because the requirement that everyone's good is to count is compatible with the good of some counting very little. To that extent, Rawls's conception of reasonableness is at odds with some aspects of existing international human rights law, including the right against discrimination on grounds of gender, religion, or race.

The root idea of the Rawlsian conception of moral authority is respect for persons' reasons in the light of what he calls "the burdens of judgment." To acknowledge the burdens of judgment is to appreciate that due to a number of factors reasonable people can disagree on the principles of public order. Like Rubin and Watson, Rawls is concerned about those who assume that their belief that certain moral principles are valid is sufficient to give them the moral authority to impose those principles on others. In that sense, Rawls's reasonableness condition is an attempt to rule out the imposition of purely personal or subjective moral views.

However, Rawls's reasonableness criterion does not rule out imposing moral standards that others do not consent to. What people *can* reasonably accept, given their moral views, and what they actually *do* accept or consent to may differ. So, according to the Rawlsian conception of moral authority (or in his preferred term, legitimacy), acts of reform that violate the state consent super-norm are not necessarily unjustifiable, even if we slide over the problem of inferring the consent of persons from the consent of states.

Rawls's conception of moral authority focuses almost exclusively on one aspect of being reasonable, or of showing respect for the reasons of others: humility in the face of the burdens of judgment. Its only acknowledgement that reasons must be of a certain quality to warrant respect and toleration is the very weak requirement of logical consistency or coherence. A quite different conception of moral authority acknowledges the burdens of judgment and also affirms that part of what it is to respect persons is to respect them as beings who have their own views about what is good and right, but places more emphasis on what might be called *epistemic responsibility* as an element of reasonableness.[29] According to this view, respect for persons' reasons does not require that we regard as reasonable any moral view that meets Rawls's rather minimal requirements of logical consistency or coherence and of taking everyone's good into account in some way. In addition, to be reasonable, and hence worthy of toleration, a moral view must be supportable by a justification that meets certain minimal standards of rationality. In other words, to be worthy of respect, moral views must be supported by reasons and reasoning that is of a certain minimal quality that goes beyond logical consistency or coherence. In particular, it must be possible to provide a justification for a moral view that does not rely on grossly false empirical claims about human nature (or about the nature of Blacks, or women, or "untouchables") and which does not involve clearly invalid inferences based on grossly faulty standards of evidence. The intuitive appeal of this more demanding conception of what sorts of views are entitled to toleration lies in the idea that respect for persons' reasons requires that those reasons meet certain minimal standards of rationality, the underlying idea being that it is respect for persons' reasoning, not their opinions, that matters. According to this conception of moral authority also, it is mistaken to assume that anyone who tries to reform the international legal system by performing acts that are violations of its existing norms is thereby imposing on others her purely personal or subjective moral views. The charge of subjectivity should be reserved for those views that do not meet the minimal standards of epistemic responsibility. Different versions of this view would propose different ways of fleshing out the idea that epistemic responsibility requires more than mere logical consistency or coherence.

My aim here is not to resolve the debate about what constitutes moral authority (though I have argued elsewhere that the epistemic responsibility view is superior to the Rawlsian view).[30] Instead, I have introduced two rival conceptions of moral authority, in order to show that both create a space between rigid adherence to existing consensual international law and the attempt to impose purely subjective, personal moral beliefs in violation of existing law. So even though it is correct to say that purely subjective or merely personal moral views cannot provide a moral justification for illegal acts of reform, it does not follow that anyone who breaks the law is merely acting on a subjective or personal view.

Watson and Rubin are quite correct to question the moral authority of proponents of illegal reform. Merely believing that one is right in itself is not a sufficient reason for doing much of anything, much less for violating the law or trying to initiate a process that will result in imposing laws on others without their consent. But they are mistaken to assume that those who advocate illegal acts of system reform must lack moral authority, and they offer no account of moral authority to show that illegal reformists must or typically will lack moral authority. In addition, as I have already argued, quite apart from whether either the Rawlsian conception of moral authority or the epistemic responsibility conception is correct, those who brand all proponents of illegal reform "subjectivists" entirely overlook the fact that in some cases, perhaps most, the reformer's justification is internalist, appealing to widely shared moral principles already expressed in the system. It does not follow that these internal values of the system are beyond criticism, but they are not purely subjective or merely personal; instead, they are widely held, systematically institutionalized values. In appealing to the internal values of the system in order to justify an illegal act, the reformer is doing precisely what reformers (as opposed to revolutionaries) do: trying to see that the system does a better job of realizing the values it already embodies and is supposed to promote. The proper lesson to draw from Watson and Rubin's worries about moral subjectivism is that the justification of illegal acts of reform must rest upon a conception of moral authority, not that no justification can succeed.

Toward a Theory of the Morality of Illegal Legal Reform

GUIDELINES FOR DETERMINING THE MORAL JUSTIFIABILITY OF ILLEGAL ACTS OF REFORM

At the beginning of this chapter, I located the problem of illegal reform in the part of nonideal normative theory of international law that deals with how we are to move toward the institutional arrangements prescribed by ideal theory.

We are now in a position to articulate some of the key considerations that such a nonideal theory would have to include. My aim here is not to offer a developed, comprehensive theory of the morality of transition from the nonideal to the ideal situation, but only to sketch some of its broader outlines so far as it addresses the problem of illegal acts of reform. To do this I will list a set of guidelines for assessing the morality of proposed illegal acts directed toward the moral improvement of the system.

The guidelines are derived from the preceding analysis of the objections to illegal acts of reform. While none of those objections rules out the moral justifiability of illegal acts of reform, they do supply significant cautionary considerations that a responsible agent would take into account in determining whether to engage in such an act. Finally, I will clarify the import of the guidelines and demonstrate their power by applying them to the recent NATO intervention in Kosovo.

An important limitation of the guidelines should be emphasized: They are not designed to provide comprehensive conditions for the justification of intervention. Instead, they are to be applied to proposals for illegal interventions once the familiar and widely acknowledged conditions for justified intervention are already satisfied. Among the most important of these familiar conditions is the principle of proportionality, which requires that the intervention not produce as much or more harm (especially to the innocent) than the harm it seeks to prevent. Much of the criticism of NATO's intervention in Kosovo focuses on the failure to satisfy this requirement. My concern, however, is with the special justificatory issues raised by the illegality of an act of intervention, understood as being directed toward system reform. To capture these justificatory issues, I offer the following guidelines.

1. Other things being equal, the closer a system approximates the ideal of the rule of law (the better job it does of satisfying the more important requirements that constitute that ideal), the greater the burden of justification for illegal acts.

2. Other things being equal, the less seriously defective the system is from the standpoint of the most important requirements of substantive justice, the greater the burden of justification for illegal acts.

3. Other things being equal, the more closely the system approximates the conditions for being a legitimate system (that is, the stronger the justification for attempts to achieve enforcement of the rules of the system), the greater the burden of justification for illegal acts.

4. Other things being equal, an illegal act that violates one of the most fundamental morally defensible principles of the system bears a greater burden of justification.

5. Other things being equal, the more likely it is that the illegal act will actually contribute to a significant moral improvement in the system, the stronger the case for committing it.

6. Other things being equal, illegal acts that are likely to improve significantly the legitimacy of the system are more easily justified.

7. Other things being equal, illegal acts that are likely to improve the most basic dimensions of substantive justice in the system are more easily justified.

8. Other things being equal, illegal acts that are likely to contribute to making the system more consistent with its most morally defensible fundamental principles are more easily justified.

THE RATIONALE FOR THE GUIDELINES

The basic rationale that is common to all the guidelines is straightforward. They provide a way of gauging (a) whether any given illegal act can accurately be described as being directed toward reform of the system and if so (b) whether committing it is compatible with a sincere commitment to bringing international relations under the rule of law.

Guideline 1 captures the idea that for those who are committed to the rule of law, the fact that a system closely approximates that ideal provides a presumption in favor of compliance with its rules. Guideline 2 is a reminder that satisfying the formal requirements of the ideal of the rule of law is not sufficient for assessing the moral quality of a legal system and hence for determining the weight of the presumption that we ought to comply with its rules. In addition to satisfying or seriously approximating the ideal of the rule of law, a legal system ought to promote justice. The elements of the rule of law supply important constraints on the sorts of rules that may be employed in pursuit of the goal of substantive justice, but they are not the only factor relevant to assessing the moral quality of the system—how well the system promotes the goal of substantive justice also matters. In the case of the international legal system, it is relatively uncontroversial to say that the most widely accepted human rights norms constitute the core of substantive justice (to call this a subjective or purely personal view would be bizarre). To the extent that the protection of human rights is an internal goal of the international legal system, the appeal to substantive justice is an appropriate consideration in determining whether illegal action is morally justifiable and cannot be dismissed as the imposition of purely personal or subjective moral views.

Guideline 3 rests on the assumption that the conditions that make the system legitimate, including preeminently its capacity to promote substantive justice within the constraints of the ideal of the rule of law, give us moral reasons to support it and that consequently we will be more reluctant, other things being equal, to violate its rules if it scores well on the criteria of legitimacy.

Guideline 4 follows straightforwardly from the fundamental commitment to supporting the international legal system as an important instrument for achieving justice. The reformer, by definition, is someone who is striving to bring about a moral improvement in the system. Accordingly, she must consider not only the improvement that may be gained through an illegal act, but also the need to preserve what is valuable in the system as it is. Guideline 5 is commonsensical, stating that how likely it is that the goal of reform will be achieved is one factor to be considered in determining whether illegality is warranted.

Guideline 6 acknowledges a fundamental tension in the enterprise of trying to develop a morally defensible system of law: On the one hand, a person who seeks to reform a legal system, qua reformer, values the indispensable contribution that law can make to protecting human rights and serving other worthy moral values; on the other hand, she appreciates that the enterprise of law involves the coercive imposition of rules and that for this to be justified the system must meet certain moral standards. What this means is that the project of trying to develop the legal system to achieve the goal of justice must be accompanied by efforts to ensure that the system has the features needed to make the pursuit of justice through its processes morally justifiable. Thus, Guideline 6 acknowledges the distinction between justice and legitimacy and emphasizes that anyone who is committed to working within the system to improve it should take the legitimacy of the system itself as an important goal for reform.

Guideline 7, like guideline 3, emerges from my criticism of those opponents of illegal reform who make the mistake of thinking that conformity with the ideal of the rule of law is all we should ask of a legal system. There I argued that whether a legal system achieves or at least is compatible with the substantive requirement of justice is relevant to determining its moral pull toward compliance. My discussion of alternative views of moral authority showed that while Watson and Rubin are correct to condemn those who would attempt to impose subjective—that is, purely personal conceptions of substantive justice on the legal system—illegal reform for the sake of improving the substantive justice of the system is compatible with recognizing a requirement of moral authority and hence with acting from moral commitments that are not subjective in any damaging sense.

Guideline 8 is also intuitively plausible. A reformer who commits an illegal act that can reasonably be expected to make the system conform better to its own best principles is acting so as to *support* the system and to that extent the presumption against acting illegally that supporters of the system should acknowledge is weaker.

A word of caution is in order. The guidelines proceed on the assumption that content can be given to the idea of improving the system morally, and they employ the notion of justice. However, they are not intended to provide a comprehensive moral theory nor to supply content for the notion of justice. They are designed to provide guidance for a responsible actor who both values the rule of law in international relations and is aware of both the system's need for improvement and the difficulties of achieving expeditious change by strictly legal means. It is inevitable that different actors may reach different conclusions about whether a particular illegal act directed toward system reform is morally justifiable, just as conscientious individuals can disagree as to whether a particular act of civil disobedience in a domestic system is morally justified. In some cases these different conclusions will be the result of different understandings of justice. But without having settled all disputes about what justice is, it is still possible to show that an actor sincerely committed to the rule of law in international relations, and who believes the existing system is worthy of efforts to reform it, can consistently perform or advocate illegal acts of reform. And it is possible to develop guidelines for responsible choices regarding illegal acts of reform.

NATO INTERVENTION IN KOSOVO, A TEST CASE

To cover a wide range of possible illegal acts of reform the guidelines must be abstract. To appreciate their value and to clarify their meaning I will apply them to NATO's intervention in Kosovo. I will assume that according to the preponderance of legal opinion, this was an illegal act. I noted earlier that two quite different justifications were given for the intervention: the primary justification offered was that the intervention was morally justified (even if illegal) as the only means of preventing major violations of human rights; the other was that the intervention was a first step toward establishing a new, more enlightened customary norm of humanitarian intervention that allows intervention without Security Council authorization. My concern in this paper is with the second justification, because it more clearly meets the description of an illegal act directed toward morally improving the system. How does this illegal act, justified in this way, fare with regard to the eight guidelines for assessing the moral justifiability of illegal acts of system reform?

It would be difficult to argue that guidelines 1, 2, or 3 weigh conclusively against NATO's intervention in Kosovo. As I have already noted, the existing system of international law departs seriously from the ideal of the rule of law, at least so far as this includes the principle of equality before the law; falls far short of satisfying substantive principles of justice, including those, such as human rights norms, that are internal to the system; and can be challenged on grounds of legitimacy because of the morally arbitrary way in which international law is often selectively applied in the interest of the stronger.

From the standpoint of guideline 4, the intervention in Kosovo initially looks problematic, simply because of the charge that its illegality consisted in the violation of one of the most fundamental principles of the system, the norm of sovereignty articulated in Articles 2(7) and 2(4) of the UN Charter, which forbid armed intervention except in cases of self-defense or the defense of other states, in cases of aggression.[31] However, guideline 4 refers to the most morally defensible fundamental norms. If the new customary norm of intervention that the illegal act is intended to help establish would in fact constitute a major improvement in the system, it would do so by restricting state sovereignty, and this implies that the norm of sovereignty in its current form is not morally defensible. In other words, the reformist rationale for acting in violation of the existing norm of sovereignty so as to help establish a new customary norm of intervention is that the existing norm of sovereignty creates a zone of protected behavior for states that is too expansive, at the expense of the protection of human rights. The more dubious is the moral defensibility of the principle of the system that the illegal act violates, the less force guideline 4 has as a barrier to illegal action. In cases where the establishment of a new norm through illegal action would constitute a major improvement *because* the existing norm that is violated is seriously defective, guideline 4 poses no barrier to illegal action. So whether guideline 4 counts for or against NATO's intervention in Kosovo depends upon whether the change the illegal act is aimed at producing would in fact be a major moral improvement in the system, which is addressed in guidelines 5 to 8.

The application of guideline 5 to the Kosovo intervention raises very interesting and difficult issues of epistemic responsibility regarding the prediction that an illegal act will in fact achieve the aim of reform. Just how likely must it be that the intervention will in fact make a contribution toward establishing a new customary norm regarding humanitarian intervention? Note that there is a connection between guideline 5 and guidelines 6 to 8, which identify some of the most important dimensions of improvement. The more significant the improvement would be, if it were to occur, the less demanding we should be regarding the likelihood of its actually being furthered by the illegal act aimed at achieving it, other things being equal. In other words, it may be justifiable to engage in an act that has relatively low probability of success in contributing to the creation of a more enlightened new norm, if success would constitute a major improvement in the system. Nevertheless, the question remains: how likely must it be that the illegal act will produce the desired results?

Recall that the act in question is aimed at the establishment of a new customary norm and that the process by which new customary norms are created is a complex, multi-staged one in which there are many opportunities for failure. Above all, it is important to remember that whether a new customary norm of intervention will arise will depend not just upon what NATO did in this case, but upon whether a stable pattern of similar interventions comes about, upon whether states persistently dissent from the propriety of such interventions, and upon whether those who contribute to establishing a stable pattern of similar interventions do so in a way that satisfies the *opinio juris* requirement. Given these inherent uncertainties of the effort to bring about moral improvement through the creation of a new customary norm, an actor contemplating an illegal act of reform of this sort should be on very firm ground in judging that the new norm would in fact be a major improvement. In the next subsection I will argue that this demand was not met in the case of NATO's intervention in Kosovo.

It is tempting to assume that from the standpoint of substantive justice, the Kosovo intervention scores high because the establishment of a norm authorizing intervention into internal conflicts to prevent massive human rights violations would constitute a major improvement in the system. Moreover, the charge of subjectivism (lack of moral authority) rings hollow in this sort of case because, as Kofi Annan suggested, the protection of human rights is a core value that is internal to the system. However, whether or not the NATO intervention can be described as an act of illegal reform that would, if successful, bring about a major improvement in the system depends upon the precise character of the norm that this illegal act is likely to contribute to the establishment of—and upon whether a norm of this character would be likely to be abused.

WHAT SORT OF NEW NORM OF CUSTOMARY LAW?

From the standpoint of its justifiability as an illegal act directed toward improving the system, just how the illegal act is characterized matters greatly. It is not sufficient to characterize the NATO intervention as an act directed toward establishing a new norm of humanitarian intervention in domestic conflicts. Such a characterization misses both what makes the act illegal and what is supposed to make it an act directed toward improving the system by helping to establish a new norm of intervention: the fact that it was undertaken without UN authorization. Those who endorse the act, not simply as morally justifiable, but as an act of reform calculated to contribute to the creation of a new norm, are committed to the assertion that the requirement of Security Council authorization is a defect in the system. And the fact that the intervention proceeded without Security Council authorization is the chief basis for the widely held view that the intervention was illegal.

For purposes of evaluating the justifiability of the NATO intervention as an illegal act directed toward reforming the system, then, the characterization of the act must at least include the fact that it occurred without Security Council authorization. But something else must be added to the characterization: the fact that the intervention was undertaken by a regional military alliance whose constitutional identity is that of a pact for the defense of its members against aggression. Those who undertook the intervention and their supporters emphasized that it was conducted by NATO, presumably because they thought that this fact made the justification for it stronger than would have been the case had it been undertaken by a mere collection of states. Note that this appeal to the status of NATO as a regional defensive organization recognized by international law cannot refute the charge of illegality. According to Article 51 of the UN Charter, military action, including action by regional organizations as identified in Article 52, is permissible without Security Council authorization only in cases of the occurrence of armed attack against a state or a member of such an organization.[32] So the question remains: would a new customary norm permitting regional military organizations, or those that qualified as such under Article 52, be a moral improvement in the international legal system?

The answer to this question is almost certainly negative. A military alliance such as NATO is not the sort of entity that would be a plausible candidate for having a right under international law to intervene without UN authorization. The chief difficulty is that such a norm would be too liable to abuse. To appreciate this fact, suppose that China and Pakistan formed a regional security alliance and then appealed to the new norm of customary law whose creation NATO's intervention was supposed to initiate to justify intervening in Kashmir to stop Hindus from violating Muslim rights in the part of that region controlled by India. It is one thing to say that NATO's intervention was morally justified as the only way of preventing massive human rights violations under conditions in which Security Council authorization was not obtainable. That justification for illegality makes no claims about the desirability of a new rule concerning intervention and is quite consistent with the view that despite its defects the rule requiring Security Council authorization is, all things considered, desirable under present conditions. The justification we are concerned with makes a stronger and much more dubious claim, namely, that the current rule requiring Security Council authorization ought to be abandoned and replaced with a new rule empowering regional defense alliances to engage in intervention at their discretion. Perhaps the current rule of intervention ought to be rejected, but it is very implausible to hold that adopting this new rule would be an improvement.

To conclude that the NATO intervention looks dubious from the standpoint of guidelines 5 to 8, then, is an understatement. The problem is not just that the change in customary law that the NATO intervention was supposed to contribute to is not a sufficiently important improvement to justify violating a fundamental norm of the system, but that it is very doubtful that this change would be an improvement at all. In other words, the NATO intervention fails even to meet the threshold condition of being a plausible candidate for an illegal act of reform. So even if it scored better than it does on the other guidelines, the illegality of the act cannot be excused by appealing to the need to reform the system.

I conclude that the morality of the NATO intervention in Kosovo, understood as an illegal act directed toward improving the international legal system, is extremely doubtful. This criticism is valid independently of the cogency of the most widely publicized objection to the intervention, the charge that it violated the principle of proportionality that any intervention, legal or illegal, should satisfy because instead of stopping the ethnic cleansing of Albanians it actually accelerated it.

Conclusions

My chief aim in this paper has been to identify, and to begin the task of developing a solution for, an important but neglected problem in the nonideal part of normative theory of international law: the justification of illegal acts aimed at morally improving the system. I have also shown the inadequacy of a simple and common response to the problem—the charge that such acts are impermissible because they are inconsistent with a sincere commitment to the rule of law or betray a willingness to act without moral authority by imposing purely personal or subjective views of morality. By exploring the complex array of factors that are relevant to determining whether an illegal act of reform is morally justified, I hope to have vindicated the concerns of those such as Watson and Rubin that such illegalities bear a serious burden of justification, while at the same time showing that to reject illegal reform out of hand is to fail to appreciate the complexities of the issue.[33] This seemingly narrow inquiry has had a valuable result of much greater significance: Facing the problem of the justification of illegal reform head-on, rather than pretending that reform efforts are legal by stretching the concept of legality, forces us to probe more deeply into the nature of the international legal system and the conditions for its legitimacy.

Notes

1. Thomas Franck, "The Emerging Right to Democratic Governance," *American Journal of International Law* 86 (1992): 46-91.

2. For a valuable critical exposition of the different ways of formulating the democratic peace hypothesis, the evidence for it, and the criticisms of it, see Bruce Russett, *Grasping the Democratic Peace: Principles for a Post-Cold War World* (Princeton, NJ: Princeton University Press, 1993).

3. J.S. Watson, "A Realistic Jurisprudence of International Law," *The Yearbook of World Affairs* (1980): 265-85; Alfred P. Rubin, *Ethics and Authority in International Law* (Cambridge: Cambridge University Press, 1997) esp. 70-206.

4. There may, however, be domestic legal and/or repercussions.

5. As an example of an illegal act directed toward reform that is not an act of intervention, consider the US's unilateral declaration in 1976 of a prohibition against using fishing nets that are dangerous to dolphins in a 200-mile zone (far exceeding its territorial waters). The morality of such illegal acts directed to reform an international law in the name of protecting species or environmental protection is an important topic that merits a separate treatment.

6. The foregoing picture of international law's limited resources for lawful moral reform is, of course, a sketch in broad strokes. There are more subtle modes by which international law can be changed. For example, judicial bodies (such as the International Court of Justice) or quasi-judicial bodies (such as the UN Human Rights Committee) can achieve reforms under the guise of interpreting existing law. However, as a broad generalization it is fair to say that these modes for effecting moral improvements are both limited and slow.

7. H.L.A. Hart, *The Concept of Law* (Oxford: Oxford University Press, 1961) 77.

8. Watson 271-72; Rubin 124.

9. The Nuremberg Code, which prohibits experimentation on human subjects without consent, was drafted as a direct result of the prosecution of the Nazi doctors for their inhumane experiments on unwilling human subjects. Nuremberg Military Tribunals (1949) 181-82. William J. Bosch, *Judgment on Nuremberg: American Attitudes Toward the Major German War-Crimes Trials* (Chapel Hill, NC: University of North Carolina Press, 1970).

10. Rubin 97-130; Reginald Coupland, *The British Anti-Slavery Movement* (London: Oxford University Press, 1993) 151-88. Note that in adducing this example, I am not assuming that the motives of the British government were pure, only that one justification for the forcible disruption of the transatlantic slave trade that could have been given was that these illegal actions would contribute toward a moral improvement in the international legal system. Whether those who instigated the policy of disrupting the transatlantic slave trade were motivated by humanitarian concerns or not is irrelevant.

11. Watson 269-70.

12. I am indebted to Fernando Teson for clarifying this point (personal communication).

13. Lon L. Fuller, *The Morality of Law* (New Haven, CT: Yale University Press, 1964) 33-39.

14. The problem of achieving greater equality among states is a complex one. One cannot assume that the best or only way to achieve greater equality is by greater democratic participation in the making and application of international law. One alternative would be a system of constitutional checks on actions of more powerful states. For example, international norms specifying when humanitarian intervention is justified might be crafted to reduce the risk that powerful states would abuse them, by requiring very high thresholds of human rights abuses before intervention was permitted, and by requiring international monitoring of the process of

intervention to facilitate ex post evaluation of whether the requirement of proportionality was met, etc. I am indebted to T. Alexander Aleinikoff and David Luban for emphasizing this point (personal communications).

15. Henry Shue, *Basic Rights*, 2nd ed. (Princeton. NJ: Princeton University Press, 1980) 131-52; Thomas Pogge, "An Egalitarian Law of Peoples," *Philosophy & Public Affairs* 23.3 (1994): 195-98.

16. There are two quite different conceptions of legitimacy that are often confused in the writings of political theorists. The first, weaker conception is that of being morally justified in attempting to exercise a monopoly on the enforcement (or the making and enforcement) of laws within a jurisdiction. The second, stronger conception, often called "political authority," includes the weaker condition but in addition includes a correlative obligation to obey the entity said to be legitimate on the part of those over whom jurisdiction is exercised. I have argued elsewhere that it is the former conception, not the latter, that is relevant to discussions of state legitimacy in the international system. I would also argue that this is true for legitimacy of the system. Allen Buchanan, "Recognitional Legitimacy and the State System," *Philosophy & Public Affairs* 28.1 (1999): 46-78.

17. Watson can perhaps be interpreted as endorsing this version of the Fidelity to Law Argument. He strongly emphasizes that international law will only be effective in constraining the behavior of states if it is consensual and rejects illegal acts of reform as being incompatible with the requirement of consent. See Watson 265, 270, 275. The chief difficulty with this line of argument is that while it would be extremely implausible to say that there must be perfect compliance with law for it to be effective, Watson does nothing to indicate either what level of compliance is needed for effectiveness or what counts as effectiveness.

18. Rubin 190-91, 205, 206; Watson 265, 270, 275.

19. The literature exposing the deficiencies of the various forms of Realism in international relations is voluminous. Of particular value are Charles Beitz, *Political Theory and International Relations* (Princeton, NJ: Princeton University Press, 1979) 3-66 and writings of the liberal theory of international relations by Anne-Marie Slaughter ("International Law in a World of Liberal States," *European Journal of International Law* 6.4: 503-38) and Andrew Moravcsik "Taking Preferences Seriously: A Liberal Theory of International Politics," *International Organization* 51.4 (1997): 513-53.

20. Terry Nardin, *Law, Morality, and the Relations of States* (Princeton, NJ: Princeton University Press, 1983) 5-13; John Rawls, *The Law of Peoples* (Cambridge, MA: Harvard University Press, 1999) 51-120.

21. Nardin acknowledges that states do share some ends, for example the flourishing international trade, but his view seems to be that what is distinctive about international law is that it binds together states in the absence of shared substantive ends.

22. Watson 268.

23. For a valuable exposition and defense of the idea of a global culture of human rights, see Rhoda E. Howard, *Human Rights and The Search for Community* (Boulder, CO: Westview Press, 1995) 1-20.

24. Fernando Teson, *The Philosophy of International Law* (Boulder, CO: Westview Press, 1998) 39-41.

25. Benedict Kingsbury, "Sovereignty and Inequality," *European Journal of International Law* 9 (1998): 599-625.

26. Kofi Annan, Speech to the General Assembly, 20 September 1999: 2 (20 Sep 1999; SG/SM/7136 GA/9569: Secretary-G).

27. John Rawls, *Political Liberalism* (New York: Columbia University Press, 1993) 136-37.

Contrib

JOVAN BABIC is Professor of Ethi[
author of *Kant and Scheler* (1986) a
published numerous articles in pr[
ethics — especially Kantian ethics —

ALLEN BUCHANAN is Professor o[
University, Durham, North Caro[
Bioethics and Political Philosophy
theory). He is the author of several
Political Divorce (1991) and *Justice,*
Foundations for International Law (f

ANTHONY ELLIS was Senior Lect[
Moral Philosophy Department at th
fore becoming Professor of Philoso[
He was also co-founder and first aca[
and Public Affairs in St. Andrews.
areas of philosophy, including ae[
of religion, philosophy of law, eth
Ethics and International Relations (1[

ALEKSANDAR JOKIC is Professor [
Director of the Center for Philos[
College, and co-founder with Jovar
Conference Series (ILECS). He is
(1996), editor of *War Crimes and*
History to Justice (2001), and co-e[
and Reference (2003) and *Consciousr*

28. Allen Buchanan, "Justice, Legit
Liberalism, ed. Victoria Davion and (
Publishers, 2000) 73-89.

29. Thomas Christiano, "On Rawls's
Buchanan, *Justice, Legitimacy, and Self*
Law (forthcoming, Oxford University F

30. Buchanan, "Justice, Legitimacy a
Determination.

31. For a valuable review of the evide:
manitarian intervention, even with Secu
"Changing Conceptions of Interventio
Intervention (a collection of essays from
Sciences), ed. Laura W. Reed and Carl K
Security Studies, American Academy of

32. Barry E. Carter and Phillip R. Tri
Little, Brown, 1995) 14-15.

33. I am indebted to David Miller, Be:
for their astute and constructive comme
Avery Kolers of the University of Arizon
Luban, Jane Stromseth, and other memb
University Law Center for their extreme
sion of this paper.

His most recent published papers deal with issues in Kantian ethics, the morality of economic sanctions, fetal rights, and ethics of international activism.

MICHAEL PHILIPS is a Professor of Philosophy at Portland State University. His work has appeared in *Mind*, *The Philosophical Quarterly*, *The American Philosophical Quarterly*, *Philosophical Studies*, *Ethics*, *Nous*, and other journals. His work has appeared in nine anthologies. His book, *Between Universalism and Skepticism*, was published by Oxford University Press in 1994. He is currently a frequent contributor to the English magazine *Philosophy Now*.

THOMAS POGGE is a Professor of Philosophy at Columbia University where he teaches moral and political philosophy. His recent publications include *World Poverty and Human Rights* (Polity Press 2002); *Global Justice* (Blackwell 2001); "What We Can Reasonably Reject" (*Nous* 2002); "On the Site of Distributive Justice" (*Philosophy and Public Affairs* 2000); and, with Sanjay Reddy, "How Not to Count the Poor" (www.socialanalysis.com). Pogge's work was supported, most recently, by the John D. and Catherine T. MacArthur Foundation and the Princeton Institute for Advanced Study. He is spending the 2002-03 academic year at All Souls College, Oxford.

ALFRED P. RUBIN is Distinguished Professor of International Law at The Fletcher School of Law and Diplomacy, Tufts University, Massachusetts. From 1994 to 2000 he was President of the American Branch of the worldwide International Law Association. He is the author of about 100 articles on a wide variety of topics dealing with international law and the author of four books, the latest of which is *Ethics and Authority in International Law* (1997), which is critical of current efforts to establish an international criminal court.

BURLEIGH WILKINS is a Professor of Philosophy at the University of California in Santa Barbara. He has made a substantial contribution to the analytic philosophy of history and the study of Burke's political philosophy. He is the author of *Terrorism And Collective Responsibility* (1992), *Hegel's Philosophy Of History* (1974), and numerous journal articles including "A Third Principle Of Justice," *Journal of Ethics* (1997).